India's and China's Missing Girls

Gwendolyn Simpson Chabrier

ATLANTIC
PUBLISHERS & DISTRIBUTORS (P) LTD

Published by
ATLANTIC
PUBLISHERS & DISTRIBUTORS (P) LTD
7/22, Ansari Road, Darya Ganj, New Delhi-110002
Phones : +91-11-40775252, 40775214, 23273880, 23275880
Fax : +91-11-23285873
Web : www.atlanticbooks.com
E-mail : orders@atlanticbooks.com

Branch Office
5, Nallathambi Street, Wallajah Road, Chennai-600002
Phones : +91-44-48531784, 28411383
E-mail : chennai@atlanticbooks.com

Printed in India at Nice Printing Press, A-33/3A, Site-IV,
Industrial Area, Sahibabad, Ghaziabad, U.P.

With love, to Dog and to all my four-legged children:
Sterling Silver Simpson, Andrea Heloise, Bebe',
Junioress and Napoli.

Preface

For centuries the patriarchal and often openly sexist attitude so deeply rooted in both Indian and Chinese culture has been confining women in a limbo of precariousness, ignorance and exploitation. Seen, from time to time, as an evil and lascivious temptress or as a burden too heavy for the family to be carried, the "other half of the sky" has been historically relegated to the two archetypical roles of prostitute and slave, both of which vilifying her as a creature whose only purpose was to serve men. No more dignified than simple commodities, women's very own right to life has too often and too easily been denied: sex-selective abortions and female infanticide are plagues still riding Indian and Chinese societies, though many government schemes and programs have been implemented in both countries to stem and possibly eradicate the phenomena. Even their abandonment as infants has proved to be a lucrative business for scrupleless adoption agencies eager to sell baby girls at high prices to Western desperate childless couples, as well as for appalling traffickers fueling and exploiting the prostitution market.

Through accurate historical surveys, first-hand testaments, official sources and international reports and data, *India's and China's Missing Girls* vividly and thoroughly portrays the exploitation, commodification and castigation of women of all ages in India and China, together with its ultimate result: the progressive rarefaction of female presence inside society and the dramatic sex-imbalance now mining the very roots of a regular social life. Only the consistent, even though relatively recent, and continuous efforts of the political establishment of the two countries can spread a new consideration, and thus a new consciousness, of the innate value of female citizens and the fundamental role they have always been playing in society.

Gwendolyn Simpson Chabrier

Contents

Chapter 1

Patriarchy in India: Child Marriage, the *Devadasi* System, Child Labor, Child Trafficking and Other Issues

INDIA'S PATRIARCHY

Women and their female progeny have been the victims of India's patriarchal system for centuries. Sanctified by Hinduism and legalized by Manu, it was a woman's *karma* to be equated with a slave, while a man was to be venerated by her like a saint, both in this life and the next. According to Manu, a man conquers the world by the birth of a son; he enjoys eternity by that of a grandson; and the great-grandfather enjoys eternal happiness by the birth of a grandson's son (Prabhu 242). Her subservient role could and still can be witnessed in the home, at work or in the community at large. She must and is still striving courageously for her merited equality. India has become increasingly more conscious of the disparity between the sexes and the castes and through focusing on education and legislation the country is beginning to seriously address the flagrant inequality and injustice toward women and her girl children, in particular, Charles Fourier once remarked that a civilization could only be judged by the social and political position of its women. If this is true, one can only hope that Indian women will recover their former state accorded to them in ancient India, similar to the one enjoyed by women in ancient China. The women's movement and the numerous women's organizations such as SEWA are all devoting themselves to the needs and demands of the broad spectrum of Indian women throughout the country. They are demonstrating that women's gradually improved educational and economical status are the vehicles by which they and the next generation will attain their empowerment and self-esteem, the psychological conditions necessary for their advancement and their upliftment.

Despite the fact that there are various theories about the beginnings of the Hindu caste system, it is generally agreed that the Vedic Aryans with their fair skin and chiseled features entered initially into Northern India through the Hindu Kush. Their invasions began around 1500 B.C. and lasted for a couple of hundred years. It was during this period that they were deemed to have created the *varna* system. These Sanskrit-speaking Aryan conquistadors from Southern Europe and Northern Asia, highly militant according to the *Vedas,*[1] were assisted by their gods, such as the fire-breathing Agni, not to mention the thunder bolt throwing Indra. They were alleged to have made dramatic entries into India on their horse-drawn chariots and to have conquered the country's dark aborigines who, because of their color, were alluded to as the *dasa* or *dasyus* both in the *Vedas* and in the *Manusmriti.*[2] The Aryans subjugated the natives, mainly Dravidians, throughout the Indus Valley and Punjab and continued their conquest as far east as the plains of Delhi. Meanwhile, these dark, flat-nosed, uncivilized *dasa*, when not enslaved or placed into serfdom, which was often the case, fled to the mountains or jungles, if not to the South.

These semi-nomadic Vedic conquerors quickly found it necessary to structure the new world to which they had immigrated. Simultaneously, they were also motivated to enforce their supremacy and their racial purity and to perpetuate it. Most importantly, the caste system that they were to create was in complete accordance with their religion, given the *varna* system formed an integral part of the Vedic texts. According to

1. The four *Vedas* were sacred texts written in Sanskrit between 1500 and 1000 B.C. They contained the first written accounts of the Indian people and their culture.
2. The *Manusmriti* (Manu's code of law) was written around 1500 B.C. It sanctioned the caste system and the debasement of women and the lower castes.

the *Purushasukta*, one of the later hymns of the *Rig Veda*,[3] after Purusha's[4] sacrifice to the gods, the four *varnas* were created from the different parts of his body: the Brahmins from his thousand heads, the Kshatriyas from his arms, the Vaishyas from his thighs, and the Sudras from his feet. The caste hierarchy was determined by the descending order of the diverse organs from which the *varnas* were issued. Likewise, the Vedic chants were also first created through his sacrifice.

Hindu society developed into a four-tier hierarchy where the Brahmins, the priestly and the learned were at the top. They were followed by the Kshatriyas, which included the warriors, the nobility and the politicians. In succession were the Vaishyas, the merchants and the landlords. The Sudras occupied the bottom of the ladder. They were the peasants, farmers, artisans and craftsmen, to list a few, whose duty was above all to serve the upper castes who even today consist of not more than 15% of the population. These four *varnas* were referred to as *savarna*. Concurrently, the Untouchables were outside of the system and were described, by contrast, as *avarna*, meaning without a caste. They were treated as outcastes mainly because they were deemed impure, usually as a consequence of their professions, which were considered polluting. They were often corpse bearers, caretakers of the cremation grounds, leather tanners, latrine cleaners, scavengers, shoemakers or street cleaners.

The men of the first three castes were distinguished as *dvijas* or 'twice-born'. This meant at the age of eight, eleven, or twelve, a young Hindu underwent a second birth, this time a spiritual one. He was invested with a sacred thread[5] and initiated into the mysteries of Hinduism. It was at this time, he was admitted to the study of the *Vedas* and other sacred texts.

3. The *Rig Veda* is a collection of 1,028 hymns which is the first of the four *Vedas*. It is the world's oldest book, written around 1500 B.C. It reveals the origins of the caste system and the Untouchables.
4. Primal man.
5. According to the Laws of Manu, the sacred thread of a Brahmin was made of cotton, that of a Kshatriya of san (hemp or flax) thread and that of a Vaishya of woolen thread. Again, distinctions were made between castes.

Women, independent of their caste, Sudras or Untouchables remained 'once-born' and by Hindu tradition were not allowed access to the holy writings or to any other amenities of their religion. Initially, they were not even given the possibility of an improved status in another re-incarnation. According to Manu:

> **XI. 36-37.** A woman shall not perform the daily sacrifices prescribed by the *Vedas*. If she does it, she will go to hell.

In Hinduism, women, additionally, have always been regarded less pure than men, simply because defilement has always been connected mainly with menstruation, childbirth and, to some extent even to widowhood. Additionally, there has always been less difference between purity and impurity in the lower castes because lower caste women, unlike their purer caste counterparts, have been forced to earn a livelihood. Whether working in the fields, in midwifery, in dirt disposal or in housekeeping, just to cite a few, these women have been considered more exposed to pollution.

In ancient times, prior to Manu not only were women free to choose their husbands or if widowed to remarry, they also held a position of high respect in the intellectual and social life of the country. Like the men, it is evident through the *Shranta Sutras* that women repeated the *mantras* of the *Vedas* and that they were also taught to read them. They furthermore attended college; many became teachers who in turn taught the *Vedas* to their female students. They were also renowned for their capability of maintaining discussions with men on very complex subjects pertaining to religion, philosophy or metaphysics, as examples. Ambedkar, the most eminent of the Scheduled Caste leaders, believed that these laws which disabled the women and the Sudras in particular, were imposed upon them since they were considered the two principal groups in Aryan Society who were seeking refuge in the Buddhist faith. Consequently, they were undermining the Brahminic religion and needed to be controlled.

Through examining certain of the laws in the *Manusmriti*, one understands to what degree women, and by extension the girl child, were debased and why they are concurrently still struggling to regain their initial respect and equality; the Untouchable and Sudra women of course being the most vulnerable, as they were positioned at the lowest level of the social, economic and religious ladder. According to Manu:

> **II. 213.** It is the nature of women to seduce men in this (world); for that reason, the wise are never unguarded in (the company of) females.
>
> **II. 214.** For women are able to lead astray in (this) world not only a fool, but even a learned man, and (to make) him a slave of desire and anger.

In a word, Manu depicted a woman as an evil, seductive temptress who was deleterious to men. Thus, at all times she must be kept captive by men and allowed no independence. Not only was she to be subject either to her father, husband or sons, but also Manu asserted:

> **V. 147.** By a girl, by a young woman, or even by an aged one, nothing must be done independently, even in her own house.
>
> **V. 149.** She must not seek to separate herself from her father, husband, or sons; by leaving them she would make both (her own and her husband's) families contemptible. Woman is not to have a right to divorce.

For Manu, a woman was to be totally appendaged to a man, signifying that she was completely under his control. Regarding divorce, it is important to clarify that in reality, a married man was still free, while it was only the woman who was bound to her husband. A wife was, for all intense purposes, her husband's slave.

> **IX. 46.** Neither by sale nor by repudiation by her husband is a wife released from her husband.

Since she was initially her husband's property, whether he sold or repudiated her, according to Manu, she was always beholden to him and could never become the legitimate wife of another man who had bought her or who was simply involved with her. A wife was furthermore reduced to a slave by the *Manusmriti* also in matters of property:

> **IX. 416.** A wife, a son and a slave, these three are declared to have no property; the wealth which they earn is (acquired) for him to whom they belong.

Under the *Manusmriti*, the husband was furthermore allowed to beat his wife:

> **VIII. 299.** A wife, a son, a slave, a pupil and a younger brother of full blood, who have committed faults, may be beaten with a rope or a split bamboo.

Finally, Manu enthralled India's women, particularly the lower caste ones in a male patriarchal system, one sanctioned by religion, where a woman's husband, despite his frequent and accepted bigamy, was her God:

> **V. 154.** Though destitute of virtue, or seeking pleasure elsewhere, or devoid of good qualities, yet a husband must be constantly worshipped as a God by a faithful wife.

Indian women, particularly those of the lower castes, centuries later are still struggling relentlessly to free themselves from Manu's fetters.

This imposed admiration for men, sanctioned as far back as Manu, is also manifested even in some of the Dalits' religious practices. In Mahar, for instance, the lower castes women fast bi-yearly for the sake of their husbands and they celebrate *Vat Savitri* in May/June by walking seven times around a banyan tree, worshipping it while they pray for the "grace to be married seven times to the same husband".

An article in 2010 appearing in *The Economist* referred to the preponderance of the male population as a result of 'gendercide', due to abortions, where many of the baby girls are simply killed off. The rationale for this is purely economical. Not only do boys earn more than girls, but also India, like most of China, lacks any universal pension system and sons are expected to pay for their aged parents. Until fairly recently, it was also automatic that they inherited the family business and wealth. In the past, in royal families, primogeniture was practiced, however, in the rest of society, sons inherited equally. Now, although daughters have the right to inherit like in China, they still often need the courage to defend these rights and win in one of the country's high courts. A couple of decades ago, the bride price was replaced by the dowry. Thus, girls are also viewed as a financial liability, since they require a dowry and a wedding, customarily paid by their parents. In relative terms, the dowry is often expected to be quite substantial. In the upper castes and among the wealthy and educated, the girl's parents are often expected to buy the boy a business, an apartment or maybe a car. In the lower castes and among the poorer and uneducated, the girl's family might, for instance, make a contribution to the boy's education, or give his family jewelry or cattle. Meanwhile, the girl lives with the boy's parents, so gives nothing to her natal family. In Delhi, in the first half of 2010, there were as many as sixty-six registered dowry deaths, meaning that the bride was murdered by her in-laws because her dowry was considered insufficient. Although dowry deaths tend to be more frequent among the higher castes, suicide or attempted suicide occur more frequently among the Harijan brides. Mostly, these girls burn themselves with kerosene. It is also habitual that when these young brides are brought to the hospital initially, they pretend that their burns were the result of a cooking accident. However, the greater part of these deaths certainly remains unregistered and the number must be considerably higher.

By 1994, since abortions of baby girls had already become so rampant, the government passed the PSPNDT Act (Pre-Natal Diagnostic Techniques Act) in order to prohibit the eight-dollar ultrasound tests which predetermined gender. However, despite the doctor jeopardizing his practice as well as risking three years imprisonment and heavy fines and the mother also being threatened with incarceration as well as hefty fees, the hundred-million-dollar business remains thriving. There are ultrasound shops all over India, many in the marketplaces, many of them resembling other bodegas. One sees long lines of pregnant women waiting outside these shops with misleading signs stating "Here prenatal sex determination (boy or girl before birth) is not done. It is a punishable act." Upon entry it is unnecessary to fill out insurance forms, but a woman has to sign a form that states: "I do not want to know the sex of my fetus." She also has to write down the number of children she currently has as well as their sex. However, very recently, the laws have become more and more stringent and the woman has to provide an identity card or one belonging to her husband or another member of her immediate family. In many sonography centers tracking devices, which are called 'silent observers' are now also being used to monitor the killing of the girl children. After the test, the technician often responds to the mother in code by writing the result either with a pink or a blue pen. Otherwise, if it is a boy, he might tell her to "celebrate with sweets" where if it is a girl, he advises her to "begin to put money away.", alluding, of course, to her dowry. In fact, at the birth of a boy there is often a big celebration while the birth of a girl tends often to resemble a funeral wake. Finally, abortions are also performed at home. Women buy packs of mifepristone and misoprostol which allow them to miscarry without any harmful side effects and not even a prescription is necessary for these ten-dollar abortions. Otherwise, while the higher castes use these tests, they are too expensive for the lower ones, so they tend instead to patiently await the long-expected sons.

Apart from the pre-natal diagnostic tests, today there are numerous books for sale on the subject such as *Gender Selection: Learn How to Conceive a Boy or Girl.* Such a book claims to teach a couple how diet or even the 'right' sexual position can influence the gender of a newborn. This literature is but the tip of the iceberg: the Internet proliferates with sites, forums and blogs giving advice, almost inevitably with no scientific foundations, on how to conceive the 'right' baby, that is a baby boy. All this is only a further reflection of the importance of patriarchy within Indian society.

Otherwise, throughout the world, generally, there are more boys than girls, 105 for 100. In India, today, there are 940 female births for every 1000 male births. Ten years ago, there were instead 933 girls for 1000 boys. Over the last twenty years, there have been a million missing female births or half a million per year. This problem is also graver in the North which is more patriarchal; Jaisalmer (Rajasthan) having the lowest sex ratio in the world, approximately 550:1,000 females for males born. Otherwise, for instance, in Bibipur, a small town in Rajasthan, alluded to as the village of brides, during general elections a local organization called Kunwara Union or 'Bachelors' Union', even offered their votes in exchange for wives: "Give us brides and win our votes!". Therefore, many of these men look for a wife in such regions as Kerala or Assam, where the women are more abundant, given they hold a higher status, although equally poor.

Yet, there has also been a very recent tendency in the higher caste families who only have sons, to be very content at the arrival of a daughter. While grandfathers who showed indifference at best at the birth of their own daughters now are thrilled and participate joyously with the arrival of a baby girl; their spouses are obviously unhappy that they were not shown the same attention. This notwithstanding, some girls, particularly in destitute families, are also killed upon birth. Meanwhile, and particularly in the lower castes and poorer families where the girl children have become a serious financial burden, their fathers have the proclivity of marrying them off without a dowry. For example, when there are too many daughters, they are wedded to normally unsuitable partners such as much older men, to men who are unemployed, to widowers with children, to men with physical handicaps, or simply to drunkards. A young girl can also be married off to a man who is already married despite the fact that polygamy is illegal. It is frequent that this betrothal is subject to police investigation, but, if so, the husband merely denies it by stating that he does not have the means to provide for two wives. When these women are badly treated, it is renowned that no one ever comes to their defense. These unions occur without much festivity, the girls are simply taken to the man's house and the parents are relieved that there is now someone else to provide for her. Even if they are later extremely unhappy, it is uncommon for their natal families to allow them back.

On October 26, 2006, a law was passed whereby a male could now be attacked for verbal abuse, physically abusing, beating, pushing or shoving his wife and also for sexual abuse and forcing her to have sex or looking at pornography. He can also be charged for insulting her or for economic abuse, if materially he does not provide for his wife and children. This law also includes dowry demands and threats and a man can be jailed for up to one year or fined ₹ 20,000 (480 U.S. dollars) or both for his transgressions. Unfortunately, however, a majority of the victims remain poor and illiterate lower caste women who do not read the newspapers or own radios or televisions and are thus too ignorant of their rights, if still too intimidated to defend them.

Yet, although women in general and lower caste ones in particular, have far from reached their goal of equality, over the last fifty years; they still have made definite strides in becoming part of their country's political voice. Beginning with Indira Gandhi as Prime Minister or later two Dalit women, whether Meira Kumar as Speaker of the Lower House of Parliament, or Behen Mayawati as Chief Minister in Uttar Pradesh, women are unquestionably defying Manu and making themselves heard.

Furthermore, Prime Minister Narendra Modi has been extremely conscious and empathetic to the plight of the girl child. Thus, he created the Beti Bachao, Beti Padhao Yojana (Save Girl Child, Educate Girl Child) which is a social campaign organized by the Indian Government whose goal is to generate consciousness and ameliorate the welfare services which are intended for girls. The scheme was floated with government funding of $ 16,000,000 and it is targeted particularly in the North, specifically Uttar Pradesh, Haryana, Uttarakhand, Punjab, Bihar and Delhi, areas which have a declining sex ratio (CSR). It is a national initiative which is run by the Ministry of Women and Child Development, the Ministry of Health and Family Welfare, and the Ministry of Human Resource Development. Originally, its focalization was on the multi-sector action in one hundred areas throughout India where there was a low CSR; it has now been extended everywhere within the country. Among the many other measures taken by Modi are the following: those now who give or accept dowries are publicly shamed and the informants are rewarded, the mother-in-law is given particular attention because it is usually she who decides whether her grandchild shall live, and maternity leave has been extended from twelve to twenty-six weeks for women working in a job where the workforce is more than ten people. The scheme also created conditional cash transfers, such as the Balika Samriddhi Yojana and Dhanalakshmi Scheme in order to motivate the girls' families. On a more local level, even some men are beginning to follow suit and to advantage the girl child. *The Times of India* in January 2017 recounts the contribution of Ashok Pawar, a jubilant father of a one-year-old girl. Pawar is a local barber in Kumbhephal, a small town in Marathwada's Beed, an area notorious for female feticide and infanticide. In his matchbox size barber shop, he offers free haircuts and shaving services to fathers of newborn girls for six months. His scheme has been met with great success as Ashok avidly gives his support in the desired victory for the girl child. In a country where a girl is still given less food, health care, education and even affection, Modi's scheme is crucial in assisting her empowerment and eliminating gender-based sex selective domination.

CHILD MARRIAGE

Child marriage, the *devadasi* system, child labor and child trafficking and prostitution, are illegal and punishable in India, however, with the exception of the latter which continues to augment, all remain less prevalent, less obvious but still exist today. The children who are victims of these customs are again almost inevitably from very poor, rural, illiterate families and mainly poverty and ignorance has led parents to sacrifice them to these practices. In India, child marriage began as early as the Middle Ages, however, punitive legislation only came to the fore at the end of the nineteenth century. Yet, the most significant of the early legislation was not enacted until the Child Marriage Restraint Act in 1929. It was also the first social reform issue which was addressed relentlessly by India's organized women's groups and remains one of their major concerns. Yet, it was not until more recently in 2006 that the government enacted the Prohibition of Child Marriage Act in order to prevent child marriage instead of too often only restraining it.

Initially, child marriage was non-existent in ancient India. Instead, the most popular form of marriage was *swayamvara*, where the potential grooms assembled at the house of the future bride, who chose her spouse. This form of marriage is also found in India's epics (the *Ramayana* and *Mahabharata*). Other types of marriage which occurred frequently in ancient India were either *gandharva viviha* (love marriage) or *asura viviha* (marriage by abduction). It was not until the Middle Ages, when the Sultan of Delhi came into power, that child marriage was practiced. The Hindus furthermore viewed the birth of a female child as inauspicious, and were known for drowning the baby girl in a tub of milk. Parents often opted also for early marriage, believing that it was a way to assist in the protection of their daughters' virginity, given that a young girl was constantly at the mercy of the predatory saracenic feudal lords and princelings.

During this period, India was a feudalistic society in which honor, rivalry, hereditary friendship or animosity were values which were given much significance. As a consequence, military alliances were of extreme importance in the balance of power and to ensure that these agreements were respected, often there was an exchange of young family members. They became the safeguards, a form of insurance policy that agreements would be respected between the two kingdoms or clans. The best assurance was the marriage of the two children which occurred as early as possible, so that the boy or girl was too young to contest the union. Even today, some families use child marriages to develop and strengthen relationships, to secure property transactions, to end disagreements, or to pay a debt. Equally, during wartime, parents marry their daughters in order that they may be protected from the consequent conflicts and dangers around them. Similarly, child marriage is also frequent at the time of natural disasters such as drought or tsunamis which can result in girls being sold off as brides in order to assist the rest of the family's survival.

Before the Child Marriage Restraint Act, legal prevention of child marriages began already in 1880. Instead of establishing the minimum age of marriage, social reformers chose to lobby to have husbands punished who had sexual intercourse with their spouses when they were below a particular age. Later, in 1929, the Child Marriage Restraint Act or Sarda Bill, named after its sponsor, Rai Sahib Sarda, was passed. It applied to all Indians irrespective of religion throughout the country with the exception of those residing in Jammu and Kashmir. By this law, a girl had to be at least fourteen and a boy eighteen in order to marry. If either were younger, fines and short imprisonment occurred. By the law, marriages were punishable but not made void. Although this law was intended to protect both male and female children, it was in reality discriminatory against the girl, because her marriage age was lower than the boy's. This was unlike the Muslim personal laws whereby both girls and boys could marry at the time of puberty, at fifteen years of age.

This notwithstanding, various women's groups such as the All India Women's Conference, the Women's India Association and the National Women's Conference petitioned to pressure politicians for their support of the bill. Members of the All India Women's Conference, for instance, had delegations holding up placards and threatened the public with vehemence that if they opposed Sarda's Bill, they would be ridiculed worldwide. It was also this association that was responsible for Gandhi's addressing the ills of child marriages in his speeches. Unfortunately, although the bill marked a symbolic victory for the women's movement within the country, in practice, it was still very little enforced.

In 1978, the marriage age was changed; girls had to be at least eighteen and boys at least twenty-one. This law was another step forward to discourage early child marriage. However, it was not until 2006 when the government enacted the Prohibition of Child Marriage Act, which not only restrained child marriage, but actually forbid it, that the most significant stride was made. This legislation was applicable to all Indians except the Muslims who were subject to the Islamic personal laws. By the 2006 act boys and girls forced into child marriage as minors had the option of voiding these unions during a two-year period after reaching adulthood and sometimes the marriage could even be made invalid before. All money, gifts valuables were also to be returned and the girl had to be provided with a domicile until she became an adult or marries. Furthermore, any male over eighteen who marries a minor or anyone who directs or conducts a child marriage is subject to ten years imprisonment or a heavy fine close to 4,000 rupees. In October 2017, the Supreme Court further ruled that sexual intercourse with a girl below eighteen is rape, regardless if she is married or not and she has the right to act even if the man is her husband. Any man convicted of such an act can face up to ten years imprisonment or eventually even a lifetime term. Although little of this recent legislation is not often enough put into practice, it at least demonstrates a growing consciousness which will hopefully in time liberate the young Indian girl from male supremacy.

The reasons for child marriage are multifold. In the instances where there is any property or wealth, this custom is a means by which possessions and money can be kept in the family. Often, also there is the pressure from family and community because in many rural communities early marriage is a very respected tradition. In Tamil Nadu, for instance, some villages have a strong social stigma against girls being married after puberty. Otherwise, a girl who marries as a virgin is also a means of maintaining a family's honor. Sometimes, wedlock for children is furthermore encouraged to increase the number of pregnancies in order to guarantee enough future breadwinners who will work on the family land and assist in the support of older relatives. Along with the stress placed upon a girl's fertility is also the notion that she has a shorter reproductive period in relation to a male's. For some, it is also a means of providing for a girl's future who has usually not been as well trained or educated as her masculine counterpart, and thus her future professional possibilities are much more limited. Additionally, many also feel that if a girl marries at an older age and is educated, it will be more difficult for her to assume the responsibilities of a traditional wife. Another important factor, too, is that if girls do not get married by the age of twelve to fourteen, it is difficult to find grooms for them. Often it is thought that the young women might have some form of problem which has created the delay in marriage. If they are above fifteen and have studied until this age, many think that they could have been living with other men which has resulted in the postponement of their wedding. In many cases, neither the boy nor the parents are ready to accept what they consider to be an over-aged girl. Otherwise, another disadvantage is that the girl's dowry tends to augment with a later marriage. This occurs because, as the girl gets older, she requires an older husband. An older bridegroom tends to be more educated and thus demands a higher dowry. Finally, impoverished parents also part with young daughters because of promises of marriage or by false marriage which often results in the girl becoming a prostitute abroad.

Lastly, some girls, themselves, also favor early marriages because they are aware that society is unwilling to accept unmarried pregnancies as well as sex outside of marriage. They believe that if they are not married, they are also more vulnerable to gossip. Those who have failed their school exams or who feel overburdened with heavy workloads at home hope to find an escape through early marriage.

However, despite all the justifications for early marriage, the reasons for later marriage are more justifiable. Most importantly is the fact that a girl who marries at eighteen or over, has a much better possibility to be educated and to develop both emotionally and intellectually, which further increases her self-esteem and independence. Also, if she marries as a child, she is completely at the mercy of her husband and in-laws; sexual and physical abuse being thus much more frequent.

Furthermore, the physical risks to both a mother and her offspring are also much higher for a younger bride. There is a greater danger of death and illness due to early sexual activity and child bearing. The reproductive organs are also not completely developed. Teenage mothers who are younger than eighteen, further risk hypertensive disorder, eclampsia, pre-eclampsia and post-partum hemorrhage. They are also often the victims of unsafe abortion which leads to infections, infertility and mortality, and are more likely to contract sexually transmitted diseases, as they have a greater susceptibility to hormonal fluctuations and the permeability of vaginal tissue. They are also less equipped to negotiate for safe sex. Simultaneously, their children, when they survive, are more likely to be underweight or stillborn, to suffer from malnutrition and late physical and cognitive development.

In order to encourage and safeguard the development of young girls, there are also projects which include building schools close to communities, so parents are less fearful regarding their daughter's safety, employing more female teachers, improving the relevance of their lessons, creating flexible school hours so young girls fulfill their domestic commitments, creating childcare centers within the schools, establishing penalties for male teachers who attempt to seduce girl students, and, finally, separating facilities for girls and boys.

Child marriage also creates enormous problems for child widows. If the husband dies even before consummation, the spouse is considered as a widow and is given in *nata* to a widower in her husband's family. Although she is officially his wife, under this practice, she is the property of all the men in the husband's family. If the child bride is widowed at a very young age, she can suffer from other forms of discrimination, such as the loss of status of a married female and both she and her children may lose some of their property rights. In certain cases, when girls are married very young, at five or six, for instance, and widowed a few years later, they can find themselves rejected by both their in-laws and their own families, and without any place to go.

Finally, child marriage remains most prevalent in four northern states, Uttar Pradesh, Bihar, Madhya Pradesh and Rajasthan, as well as one southern state, Andhra Pradesh. Of all these areas, Rajasthan is the epicenter where more than half the girls are married under the age of fifteen. At the time of the *Akshaya Tritiya*, a Hindu spring festival considered to be auspicious for child marriages in rural India, there is a mass celebration and solemnization of the marriage of numerous boys and girls at one time. For many girl brides, it quickly becomes a tragic event. As they are paraded in their sparkly gold and red wedding dresses, they are often found wailing out of fear and discontentment while being scolded by the priests. However, it is usually not until they are older, around fifteen or sixteen, that they actually live with their spouse. Otherwise, in this region and throughout India, in order to evade the law, child marriages are usually held clandestinely late at night. Outsiders are rarely permitted to attend these ceremonies. In the rare cases that their presence is accepted, next to never are they allowed to film the nuptial. All the villagers spend the night before the ceremony in the festivities of dancing and singing. Meanwhile, parents almost inevitably lie about the child's age, since even in the remotest village they still realize that their act is wrong. In any case, education is the key to reducing child marriage. In the Marathwada region of Maharashtra State, for instance, two years after the Health Management Pachod offered a life skills course to encourage a girl's knowledge and courage, the average marriage age grew to seventeen from fourteen and a half.

Meanwhile, the governments of Rajasthan, Karnataka and Haryana have also established an incentive program for low-income families, a majority of which are Dalit, to encourage them not to arrange marriages for their daughters until the age of eighteen. Apni Beti, Apna Dhan (ABHD), which translates to "Our daughter, Our Wealth" is one of the country's first conditional cash transfer programs to delay the marriage of young girls. In 1994, the government implemented this program in the state of Haryana. It is not an unlikely choice, given that Haryana is the state which has a very poor sex ratio according to the 2011 census (834 girls for every 1,000 boys against the national average of 918). Upon the birth of a mother's first, second or third daughter, she receives 500 rupees or $ 11 within the first fifteen days to cover her post-delivery expenses. At this time the government also gives her 2,500 rupees or $ 55 to invest in a long-term savings bond in her daughter's name which could be later cashed in for 25,000 rupees or $ 550 after her eighteenth birthday if she is not married. Apropos of this program, Anju Malhotra, whose specialization is child marriage and adolescent girls, claimed that this was the only conditional cash transfer whose focus was to delay a child's marriage and she was optimistic that this would help propel mothers to respect their daughters.

Child marriage can result in bonded labor or enslavement and commercial sexual exploitation. There are also more women than men who are the victims of child marriage and those who are forced into this practice are twice as likely to be beaten, slapped or threatened by their husbands than those who marry later, according to the International Center for Research on Women (ICRW). Although the number of child marriages has decreased from 47% in 2006 to 27% in 2016, there are still three million child marriages in India annually, 40% of the world's child marriages occurring within the country, especially among Muslims, probably due to their lower marriage age. These unions are in any case far more deleterious for girls than for boys, who are nonetheless also victimized by the tradition. The offspring of rural impoverished Untouchable families are uncontestably those who have the highest participation in child marriage, a tradition which importantly is sanctioned by Hindu culture. However, child marriage is also frequent among the higher castes, much more so than either the *devadasi* system, child labor or child trafficking and prostitution. Finally, child marriage is another custom which further reinforces the caste system, as it occurs almost inevitably within the same castes.

THE *DEVADASI* SYSTEM

The *devadasi* system or divine prostitution is a religious tradition in which young girls are 'married' and dedicated either to a god or to a temple. Ironically, even though forbidden in the *Shastras*, historically the *devadasis*, the temple dancers, have played an essential role in the Hindu temples secondary only to the priests. Even though the practice was furthermore made illegal throughout India in 1988, the custom, to a much lesser degree, still prevails but now in most cases clandestinely; punishment is also rare. Like child marriage, it is almost systematically limited to the impoverished Untouchables who find some emotional and at least minimal financial aid through dedicating a daughter to the gods.

The *devadasis*, who are often associated with the French *bayaderes* or dancers, have different names according to the region they inhabit. They are usually referred to as *joginis* in

Andhra Pradesh, or *muralis* or *jogateens* in Maharashtra. In Karnataka, they are alluded to as *basavis* and in Tamil Nadu as *thevardiyars*, to name a few. In Karnataka, the elderly *devadasis* are called *jogatis* and the young ones, *basavis*, likening them to the feminine form of a bull who roams freely around a village; an allusion to the girls' loose sexuality. They are sometimes considered as a caste or sub-caste, but the *devadasis* equate themselves instead only with a lifestyle and one which is hereditary. The tradition dates back at least to the *Puranas* in the sixth century, where there are numerous allusions to the temple dancers. Otherwise, outside of India, the practice also existed as early as 2,100 B.C. in Babylonia.

The *devadasi* system is considered to have developed originally as a result of a conflict between the feudal class and the Brahmins. The priests with their religious power over the masses managed to give prostitution a religious function. Initially, sold at private auctions, destitute low caste girls were sacrificed to temples in order to later become prostitutes. There are numerous reasons why the tradition evolved within the country. It acted as a substitute for human sacrifice and as a means to insure fertility. It was also a part of phallic worship which was an integral part of the Hindu tradition. Simultaneously, it was a way of entertaining foreigners and it served the licentious and financial interests of the Brahmins, while simultaneously justifying the exploitation of the lower classes by the upper ones.

During infancy or often between the ages of six and nine, a young girl, usually the eldest daughter, was dedicated by her parents to the local temple. If the family were of an upper caste, they would usually buy the lower caste girl and sacrifice her instead of their own child. Generally, the reasons for dedication were multifold. When the parents were very poor and could not afford the wedding expenses, if a woman was a widow and found herself pregnant and had been driven out of her home or had left it on her own accord, or in time of illness of another child when usually the mother had vowed to dedicate a daughter should the first child be cured. In fact, the first two causes were the most frequent. Otherwise, a couple also sacrificed a daughter when they had no sons. Consequently, she could not marry and became a substitute son and helped provide for the family income. Furthermore, in the case that the mother and father had some property, it was a means of safeguarding it in the family.

The dedication ceremonies varied from temple to temple and from region to region; however, all were systematically very ritualistic. In Tamil Nadu, for example, when in the first ceremony, the young girl was dedicated to the goddess, Mathamma, she was clad in a red and gold wedding dress, like the other child brides. She wore a white and red beaded necklace offered to her by the Hindu priest and as she approached the temple her dress was removed by four boys leaving her virtually naked.

The second ceremony of importance was the *devadasi* 'deflowering ceremony', which took place when she reached puberty. Often, she was sold to the highest bidder. Otherwise, whenever possible, an auspicious day was chosen. If the family had financial difficulties, they waited until they had enough money or found a man who could bear the expenses. Actually, in some cases, he who was to become her official patron had already chosen her years before at the time of her 'dedication ceremony'. In anticipation of his later position, he had already also financed the earlier expenses. Meanwhile, during the day of the ceremony, the girl was given an oil bath, and during the evening the initiatory ceremony was repeated. However, she was additionally given a sword with a lime attached to its point. The sword was placed upright on her right hand and represented the bridegroom. A tray on which a *kalasyam* (water jug or vessel) and a lamp was brought out and moved three times in front of the devotee from left to right. She then rose and carried the sword in her right hand placing it in the god's sanctuary; the ceremony ending between nine or ten at night. Most of the time, the patron who had paid for the right of deflowering the girl and spending the first night with her could also arrange a fixed sum with the mother and the grandmother in order to maintain a permanent relationship, or, if not, a limited one with the girl. Unless he specified, a long-term affair with a patron did not prohibit the *devadasi* from receiving other clients, however, when the patron arrived at her home, he always had priority over the others. These alliances were arranged and liaisons with a Muslim, a Christian or a lower caste male were forbidden. Instead, a Brahmin or a member of the upper caste was preferred for the status or wealth he could bring to the family. The children, however, could not inherit from their father.

Yet, the *devadasis* were the only women in India who learned to read, to dance and to sing. They began an arduous three-year course in singing and dancing as early as five. They often learned *sadir* (*Bharatanatyam*), *Odissi* and other classical Indian artistic traditions. Dance and music were also necessary components for the daily *pujas* in the temples. The *devadasis* lived in their mother's home near the temple where they sang and danced in the morning and evening. They also prayed and prepared food for the idol, fed him, fanned him, kept him away from the flies and put him to bed, honoring him also with sandalwood paste and jasmine garlands. Besides pampering the idol, they had other more basic duties such as distributing the water from the copper pots or replenishing the temple lamps. When individuals of importance made official visits to each other, they were always accompanied by these courtesans, otherwise it was considered discourteous. They also performed at marriages and other family functions of significance, given that they had been spared from widowhood and were consequently deemed auspicious. They were, thus, especially welcome at marriages. The guests received a string of the *tali*, prepared by them and threaded from the beads of their own necklace. Furthermore, the presence of a *devadasi* in the home of an upper caste family at the time of a religious occasion was deemed sacred and she was accordingly laden with gifts.

Otherwise, apart from being given a daily portion of rice, a *devadasi* was always paid a minimal amount of money for her services; the exact fee was determined by the size and the importance of the temple. Most temples had somewhere between eight to twelve courtesans, sometimes more. During the Chola empire, the Brihadeeswarar temple at Thanjavur boasted of four hundred dancers as well as their gurus and orchestras. In any case, after puberty and sometimes even before, the *devadasi* would supplement her income through prostitution.

Actually, in ancient times, the social status of the *devadasi* was entirely different from the degraded one it has become today. In the past, there was no stigma attached either to the *devadasi* or to her children, who were considered legitimate. The *devadasi* was considered equal to the other married women in her community. During the Sailadbhawa dynasty, the queen Kalawati had employed many *devadasis* to serve the Lord Jagannath at the Puri temple. There was a period in Orissa, for instance, when the status of a *devadasi* was highly prestigious. This was true to such an extent that even girls from rich and aristocratic families were offered for temple service. In the Middle Ages, the *devadasis* also came from some of the most prominent families in the country; the princesses of the Chola royal family being a salient example. Many were educated and in certain cases became very illustrious poets. At the time they were probably the only literate women in India. They were often also extremely wealthy as shown by their generous gifts to the temples. Otherwise, both prestige and wealth were also attached to the *devadasis* as described by Domingo Paes, a Portuguese traveler who voyaged to Vijayanagar in the early sixteenth century, before its destruction by the Muslims:

> These women are of loose character, and live in the best streets that are in the city; it is the same in all their cities, their streets have the best row of houses. They are very much esteemed and are classed among those honored ones who are the mistresses of the captains; any respectable man may go to their houses without any blame attaching there-to. These women are allowed to enter the presence of the wives of the King, and they stay with them and eat betel with them, a thing no other person may do, no matter what his rank may be.[6]

He also described their immeasurable wealth:

6. N.M. Penzer, "Poison-Damsels and other Essays" in *Folklore and Anthropology* (London: Chas. J. Sawyer, Ltd., 1952), 149-50.

> Who can fitly describe to you the great riches these women carry on their persons?—collars of gold with many diamonds and rubies and pearls, bracelets on their arms and on their upper-arms, girdles below, and of necessity anklets on their feet [...] but there are women among them who have lands that have been given to them, and litters, and so many maid-servants that one cannot number all their things.[7]

Otherwise, besides their social and economic power, they were also respected because they acted as priestesses for a few castes, especially the lower ones as they were not allowed to have priests of their own.

The *devadasi* system reached its apex during the height of the Chola empire in Southern India between the 10th and 11th century. The Brihadeeswarar temple was a typical example of the munificence of the period. The Chola kings donated thousands of *thevardiyars* to the temples they had built. The royal temples were conceived as palaces for the gods and a Chola king alone was attended by thousands of dancing girls who performed for him in rotation with the temple's gods and idols. At the beginning of the second millennium, Northern India was invaded from West Asia and many temples in the North were destroyed. Although with time the invaders moved South, there the devastation was never as great and thus the Hindu religious culture was more easily maintained. Meanwhile, later in Orissa, the Mahari culture began to decline in the 14th century with the conquest of the Sultan Shah in 1360 A.D. The Muslims imposed upon the local women the *purdah* and other restrictive customs, whereby even the *devadasis* came to lose their independence and importance.

Beginning with the first invasions in the North, the kings also lost their power and wealth, this problem being culminated with the arrival of the British. Under colonial rule, the kings, who had formerly been the patrons of the temples and the temple arts, were now completely diminished along with their

7. N.M. Penzer, "Poison-Damsels and other Essays" in *Folklore and Anthropology*, 150.

devadasis or rajadasis, those who entertained his majesty and his court. Consequently, half of the dancing girls turned to secular prostitution, while the others sought a livelihood in manual labor and agriculture. Otherwise, dancing in India and particularly under the British was associated with promiscuity and prostitution. For example, the English considered Kathak dance as a low form of entertainment and dubbed it 'Nautch dance' meaning "the dance of prostitutes". Many of these dances were performed by the *devadasis* and were closely associated with the devotional bhakti sect of Hinduism. During British rule, when many of the temple dancers became prostitutes, there was a censorship of temple dancing and finally its legal prohibition in the 1920s.

Finally, the *devadasi* system was first outlawed in 1934 through the Bombay *Devadasi* Protection Act, which outlawed the practice whether it was consensual or not. According to the act, marriage with a *devadasi* was also deemed legal and the offspring were officially legitimate. Punitive action could also be taken against anyone involved in such dedications except for the devotee herself. Those who were guilty risked a fine and up to a year imprisonment. Other clauses were also included whereby she was given some financial protection. In any case, by 1988, the custom was outlawed throughout the country, even though many of these courtesans still practice illegally.

As in the past, the *devadasis* are more prevalent in the South than elsewhere in the country. The latest statistics show close to 23,000 in Karnataka and a little over 16,500 in Andhra Pradesh. Meanwhile, Maharashtra in the Southwest has around 9,000, this number being based on the applications received for the "Devadasi Maintenance Allowance". In the meantime, Tamil Nadu, contrary to the findings of the National Human Rights Commission, claims that the system has been totally eradicated, while in Orissa there is only one remaining *devadasi* who was part of the Jagannath temple in Puri. Today, Shashimoni is over eighty-years old and swears by her virginity.[8]

8. Shashimoni, personal interview, October 23, 2011.

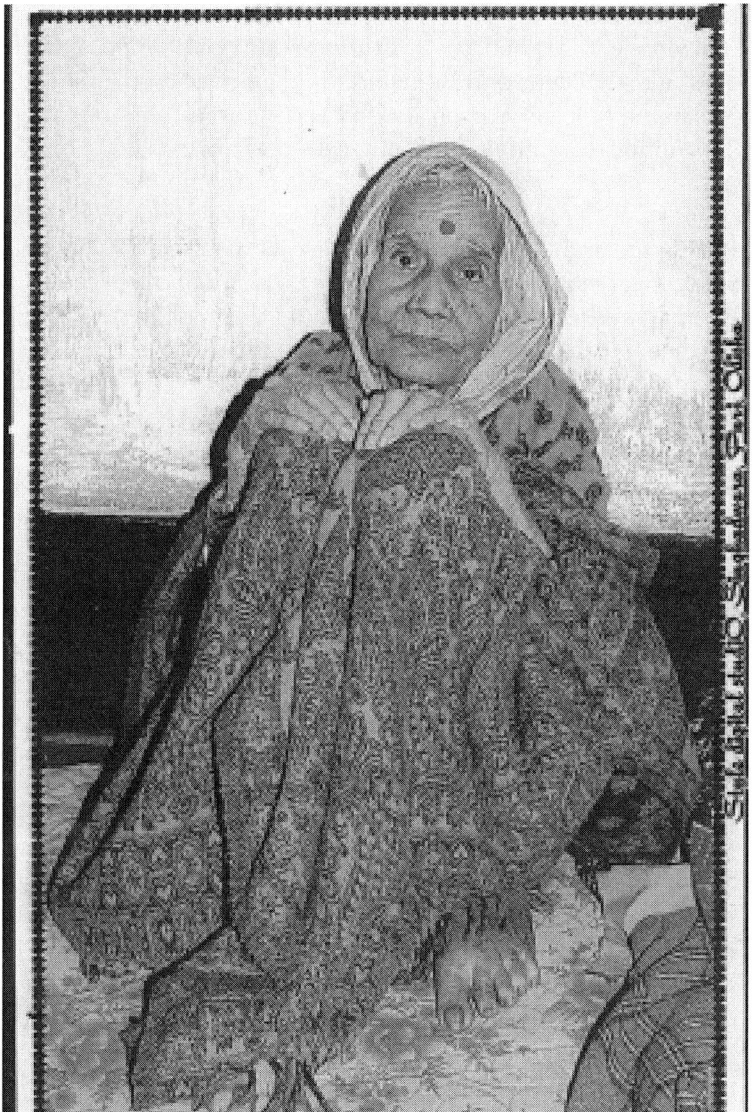

Shashimoni

Otherwise, one of the most notorious temples where the tradition still exists is a small temple, the Renuka temple, in the village of Saundatti in Karnataka. There, thousands of girls, mostly Dalits and Bahujans, are dedicated to the Goddess Yellamma twice a year on Magha and Chaitra full moon days. The family, community and other devotees march in a colorful parade singing and dancing to dedicate the young girls. The devotees of Yellamma decorate their foreheads with *haldi* (turmeric) and *kumkum* (vermilion). Sometimes they do not wear ornaments, but if they do, they usually adorn themselves with crowns, earrings and necklaces made from *cowries*,[9] which are not expensive. The atmosphere is very festive, the streets leading to the temple are carnivalesque, with many peddlers selling glass bangles, cosmetics, sweetmeats, coconuts and various and sundry items used for temple donations. Music is also heard everyplace. Otherwise, most of the time, many of the *devadasis* carry a metal vessel or a bamboo basket which they balance on their head as if it were part of their bodies. The basket or the vessel is meant to carry a brass bust, which is tastefully decorated with a great variety of flowers. They have to bathe in three holy ponds and then continue to the head priest along with other members of the family and elders of the community. The priest then gives them a lengthy sermon on how to please Yellamma. Most significantly, they are instructed that at no time during their lives are they allowed to become the wife of any one man. They are also told that they must identify with other downtrodden members of society and to assist them. Twice a week they must go begging with a *joga*, a begging bowl and visit at least five upper class families. If they, themselves, are hungry, they must not let it known and never ask for food. If they are beaten or in any way abused, they must accept it without retaliation. In a word, they are being prepared for the total submission necessary for their life as prostitutes. They also have to visit the Yellamma shrine at least twice a year on full moon days and demonstrate their devotion. During this ritual, they must be nude, preferably completely nude, or they have to cover themselves with neem foliage or minimal clothing. After

9. Sea shells.

dedication, a girl must bathe everyday early in the morning and participate in the matinal worship of Yellamma. Although she is forbidden to enter the *sancta sanctorum*, she still must bow to the deity from the outside. Afterwards, she sweeps the temple. She also learns many songs praising Yellamma and her son, Parashuram. In this village, Yellampura, as well as in certain others, the *devadasis* do not dance, but sing and play musical instruments, and recite the *Satyameva Jayate*, a mantra from the ancient Indian scripture, *Mundaka Upanishad*, while the eunuchs dance in their place. Now, a small group of them also go for yoga, from one house to another on Tuesdays and Fridays. Meanwhile, all around the lake and on the road heading to the temple, the government has placed enormous signs:

> DO NOT DEDICATE YOUR DAUGHTER. THERE ARE OTHER WAYS OF SHOWING YOUR DEVOTION.

and

> DEDICATING YOU DAUGHTER IS UNCIVILISED BEHAVIOR.

But to no avail. Today, however, the dedication occurs at night in small village temples and not always in the presence of a Brahmin priest, given that many do not want to take the risk of punishment. When they do participate, the ceremony often occurs in their homes or in a small temple in a remote village, with little visibility. They charge the family as much as 5,000 rupees. A feast is given, prayers are said and then she is presented with her *muttu*, her badge of office, and her obligations are explained to her. Otherwise, the priests and even the upper castes perpetuate the myth that if these Untouchable girls dedicate themselves to Yellamma, it will improve their *karma* and they will have the good fortune to be reborn as upper caste Brahmins.

These *devadasis* are part of the more than 450,000 who remain the victims of this practice. All of which, today, are almost inevitably Dalit, poor and uneducated. In Karnataka, for example, most come from the Scheduled Caste communities, especially the Holers, Madars and Samgars. Most are single, but

65% are associated with a patron and about 95% have children, but almost all of them are not permitted to register the names of the patron as the father of their children in the school admission records. Approximately, 63% of the young girls are forced into the system through custom, while roughly 38% are the product of families who have a history of *devadasis*. Today, unlike earlier, many are destined to become prostitutes. Nearly 40% of them join the sex trade in the cities, in particular Mumbai, while the others practice their profession in their respective villages. The majority of these girls never earn more than 1,000 rupees a month and their lives are constantly endangered by AIDS, which the *devadasis* refer to as "having the fever". By the time, a *devadasi* who does reach an age of around forty-five and is no longer considered attractive, she usually becomes a *jogathi*, an intermediary between the temple goddess and the people, or, if not, a simple beggar. Otherwise, through interviewing numerous *devadasis* and ex-*devadasis* there is a wide spectrum of reactions to their fate. While many actively engage themselves in ending the practice, a few, particularly those fortunate enough to have fallen in the hands of a protective provider laud their independence, being free of a conventional marriage.

B.L. Patil is a lawyer turned social reformer who as of now has been the single individual who has probably most assisted in aiding the victims of the *devadasi* system. Twenty-one years ago, Patil launched an organization, Vimochana, in part to avoid that the children of *devadasis* become *devadasis*, themselves. He created a school in his home in order to train them to become nurses and teachers. Today, Patil has three hundred and twenty-eight students in his school, one hundred and ten of them are children of *devadasis*. Deliberately, he mixed them with children of other backgrounds so that their later integration into mainstream society would be easier. A few children are lodged in the school and others in small houses that he has rented. Despite the criticism from individuals of the community, who are discontent to reside next to the children of prostitutes, Patil and his spouse continue relentlessly their projects. The school has thus far educated over seven hundred children and more than three hundred of them are so far married and live a normal life. Additionally, among other projects, Vimochana trains the *devadasis* in readymade garment making, in making wool yarn, blankets and mats, and in handloom weaving. Last year, Vimochana also completed a welfare project in six villages. Meanwhile, at Mallabadi, the World Bank has aided them in conserving groundwater and built tanks in order to supply water for four thousand villagers. The construction of a boys' hostel which began in 1994 is also still underway.

The *devadasi* system is a custom which is reflective of the victimization of the lower caste female which is sanctified by Hinduism and the Laws of Manu. Although much legislation has been passed in order to abolish child marriage and the *devadasi* tradition remains to a greater extent ineffective. Prisoners of poverty, lack of education, and the caste system, millions of India's young girls are still unable to escape the Hindu social religious system which has existed for centuries. A National Human Rights Commission report, published in 2006 concluded that the dedication of children continues secretly and that at least half of all *devadasis* terminate as prostitutes whether in rural or urban areas. Finally, according to the Indian Health Organization which works with former *devadasis* who are HIV-positive, at least 15,000 children are still being dedicated annually.

CHILD LABOR

After the sub-Saharan African countries, India is reputed to have the largest number of child laborers worldwide; estimates range from 60 to 115 million. In India, one out of four children between the ages of five and fifteen are employed, despite a recent widespread ban on children under fourteen working and increasing penalties for their employers. Again, the lower caste children, particularly females, who are the offspring of poor, rural families are by far the most frequent victims since poverty once again is the principal reason underlying this practice. 80% of child laborers in India are employed in the agricultural and non-formal sectors and many are bonded laborers. Most of them, particularly the girls, are illiterate or have dropped out of school after two or three years. Although Article 24 of the Constitution as well as various additional legislation prohibits child labor, like child marriage, the *devadasi* system or child trafficking and prostitution, much too often the laws go unheeded.

Despite its recent decline, child labor has existed for centuries. Before even British rule, it was already an integral part of much of Indian domestic and export trade and enterprise. Child labor has posed a problem for a long time throughout the world, particularly in developing countries. But its practice, along with its nefarious effects, are probably the most notorious in England's Victorian era. During the Industrial Revolution, children as young as four worked in production factories and, like in India, in dangerous and sometimes fatal conditions. Charles Dickens, the eminent British novelist, for instance, worked at twelve in a blackening factory while his family were in debtors' prison. Like in India, the children of poor families, during this period in England were expected to help their families financially, often working long hours in hazardous jobs for next to no pay, earning on an average 10-20% of an adult male's wage in factories, mines, and chimney sweeps.

In India, child labor is very widespread in many diverse industries, the carpet business being the best known. Otherwise, child workers are found in the glass business, the brass industry, match stick factories, brick kilns, chemical factories, gem polishing, electro-plating, lead mining, stone quarrying, rock making, the diamond industry, *beedi* production, rag picking, the garment industry, cotton seed farms, spinning mills and domestic labor; this list containing some of the principal areas but it is not all inclusive. Children are forced to work long hours and for minimal wages, if paid at all, and their health is often damaged for life, and often their survival is also in jeopardy. In most cases, their education is almost totally impeded, and their later professional possibilities become non-existent.

The Indian carpet belt, for instance, exists principally in Uttar Pradesh. There are about twenty or so loom sheds in each village. 90% of the children are bonded laborers, others are kidnapped from their impoverished villages in Bihar, the bordering state. The boys are principally low-caste Hindus while the number of girls which is steadily increasing are brought from Nepal and, in some cases, recruited to work in other states such as Rajasthan, where they work as carpet weavers. Otherwise, these young workers, many of them only eight or nine years old, are made to labor for twenty hours a day without resting. They crouch on their toes making hand knotted carpets for interminable hours and, consequently, their growth is stunted. However, the migrant children workers are subject to the worst treatment of all:

> [They are] forced to work for long hours under inhuman conditions for no wages or nominal wages. Some of them are definitely being ill-treated, beaten, tortured, abused, branded, kept half fed, without facilities or safe drinking water, medicine or rest, and are not allowed to move freely or change their employer... Four children complained that they were tied with hands folded to the legs and slung onto a jackfruit tree, then dropped on to the ground several times by pulling the rope upwards and then loosening it suddenly.[10]

Additionally, they are usually forced to sleep in the loom shed or in other cold and cramped quarters and meanwhile practically starved.

However, in this particular sector, there is a new awareness, in part due to the murder of a twelve-year-old Iqbal Masi, a bonded carpet weaver in Pakistan who was killed for leading an anti-child labor campaign. Otherwise, since the 90s, serious efforts have been made to reduce, if not eliminate, children's labor in this area. For example, for twenty years social labelling has been in existence. It consists of labelling carpets or companies by guaranteeing to buyers that the carpets for sale are made without the use of child labor.

Importantly, too, in 1990 the CWC based in Bangalore enacted the first working children's union, the Bhima Sangha, which still exists today and continues to encourage and aid the children workers to unionize and fight for their rights.

---

10. Human Rights Watch, *The Small Hands of Slavery* (N.Y., London, Washington, Brussels: Human Rights Watch, 1996), 105.

Meanwhile, in the glass business, almost all the children are employed in carrying molten glass on a seven-foot iron rod from the furnace to the adult worker and then back to the furnace, molten glass often falls on the floor, and the children can easily burn themselves; the temperature in the furnace is around seven hundred degrees centigrade. Consequently, their faces are burnt quite frequently, causing them permanent damage.

The brass industry is another area where the children workers face irremediable health problems, particularly those working in the moulding sector. The temperature in the furnace is about one thousand and one hundred degrees centigrade, and, if a drop of molten metal falls upon the child's foot, it creates an immediate hole. Furthermore, these young workers tend not to be given any breaks in their ten-hour day, and when they have the slightest lapse of concentration, they risk permanent injuries from the molten metal. Moulders are almost inevitably less than thirty years old because they become too ill to work, or are already deceased; more often than not at some point they also become the victims of tuberculosis.

Among the many other instances, child labor is very frequent among India's street children. The majority live with their parents and earn their livelihood through ten to twelve-hour days of rag picking, bringing them an income of only $ 2.50 a month, the girls always being paid less than boys. In scavenging, there is also a serious risk factor for a child's health. The children get cuts, sunstrokes, pneumonia, malaria and influenza. Often, they carry very heavy tools which stops their physical growth. They are also subject to food poisoning and digestive disorders from the leftover food. They furthermore are known to catch AIDS from the infected needles which are thrown into the garbage. Dog bites are also quite frequent since they are also scavenging for food among the heaps of refuse. The street children also meet with great difficulties on account of the local police and municipal cleaners. When any minor theft occurs, they are the first to be accused by the police. Simultaneously, the local municipal cleaners demand money and labor from them. If they refuse, the police force them to pay a higher sum. The police also require the scavengers to give over half their earnings, which is justified as a commission.

Among so many, the garment industry is another sector which is extremely hazardous for children laborers. Many work in local sweatshops and are held prisoner, locked into filthy, cramped rooms in hidden alleyways. In Mumbai, for instance, there are thousands of "sari factories", three meters by three meters rooms with dirty floors and next to no ventilation. Children aged six to fourteen labor twenty hours a day all week long, kneeling at low tables sewing colored threads and stones unto immense pieces of fabric. The children have to work, eat, wash, sleep in the same room with a tiny bathroom in one corner of the room. They are allowed two very meager meals per day.

After the recent deaths of two of the children, the Maharashtra State Government began to raid the factories and over sixteen thousand children were sent back to their villages, however, many have returned to the sweatshops. Like the carpet workers, most come from the poorest parts of Northern India such as Uttar Pradesh or Bihar, where often there are no schools in their villages or even nearby. Their families are without land to develop and when they can find work at all, their earnings do not exceed twenty to forty cents a day. When they are not kidnapped, their families often send their children back to the factories in order to supplement their meager incomes. Otherwise, there are over thirty-two thousand children missing yearly in the country, according to recent reports.

Finally, female child workers are frequently employed in spinning mills or as domestic workers. In Tamil Nadu, for instance, spinning mills in Coimbatore as well as in other areas of the state have introduced a new program entitled the *Sumangali* Scheme (marriage assistance scheme), first introduced in the late 1990s. Girls as of fourteen are recruited to work in these spinning mills. Officially, they are trained, but after a few days of training they work on a full-time basis, as the labor does not demand any previous skills. Importantly, when they are considered as trainees, they are not regarded by official sources as workers. The knitwear industry in Tirupur has also adopted this form of recruitment, extending it to girls even below the age of fourteen.

With the urbanization and the rising number of two-income middle class families, there has been an increasing demand for domestic services, particularly female child labor. Today, these families have at least one servant and three-quarters are female children under eighteen, because they are paid half the wages of their adult counterpart, receiving an average of $ 40 a month, when paid at all. Apart from the economic aspect, the children are more easily dominated and many work as much as twenty hours a day on starvation rations. In their jobs, many of them suffer sexual, physical and moral abuse. Most come from India's poorest states, many from the North, and are recruited through obscure job placement agencies, or are simply kidnapped. Consequently, there has been a notification by the Ministry of Labor by which child domestic work as well as the employment of children in *dhabas*,[11] tea stalls and restaurants are 'hazardous' occupations. The Government of India, thus expanded the Child Labor Prohibition and Regulation Act banning the employment of children employed in domestic service and in other dangerous activities, whether it be those mentioned above or additionally in hotels spas and resorts, this being effective already in 2006.[12]

Many non-governmental organizations are also seriously involved in eradicating child labor. For example, Navajeevan Bala Bhavan (NJBB) which means 'new life' is based in Andhra Pradesh, the state which has the highest amount of child labor in the country. It focuses on giving girl laborers the opportunity to study or become part of vocational program, given that girls have been more disadvantaged in India's patriarchal system.

Bonded child labor is also a widespread phenomenon in India. It began during colonial times as a means to procure reliable, cheap labor with loan and land-lease relationships, a usage of that period. It is a system of forced labor, usually full-time, but

11. Local restaurants along the highways.
12. The Child Labor (Prohibition and Regulation) Act of 1986 prohibits the employment of children below the age of 14 in hazardous occupations identified in a list by the law which was expanded in 2006 and again in 2008.

sometimes part-time whereby, the child himself, occasionally, but much more often the parents or the family as a whole enter into an agreement, usually an oral one, with a creditor, selling the child for an indeterminate period into a form of slave labor. In many cases, it occurs in order to cover certain expenses, often a social occasion such as a wedding, or else frequently an illness, otherwise the child's bondage may simply be the result of extreme poverty. Debts tend to average somewhere between $ 15 to $ 220. The children as usual are from the lowest echelons of society, such as the Scheduled Castes and Tribes. Like other forms of child labor, it occurs predominantly in the agricultural sector and other allied occupations. However, lately, it also takes place in other areas, whether *beedi*-rolling, brick kilns, carpet weaving, construction, and match factories, hybrid cottonseed production, leather, mines, quarries, silk, synthetic gems, and also prostitution, to name a few. Many of the bonded children and family labor operations today are also moving from urban factories unto rural homes. In these diverse industries, there are fifty-five million bonded child workers, as well as ten million who are relegated to the domestic sphere. These children are mainly migrant workers living far away from their families and are thus more easily exploited. Sexual and physical abuse are frequent, and sometimes even torture is not uncommon; girl children are more frequently victimized.

Apart from agriculture which employs by far the largest number of child laborers, one of the areas which is the most notorious for female bonded child labor is the *beedi* or cigarette rolling business, which is one of the twenty-five areas that the Child Labor (Prohibition and Regulation) Act deemed hazardous. Most of the *beedi* production occurs in the South, specifically in Tamil Nadu. The children work between ten and fourteen hours, six and a half days a week, with very short breaks for lunch and dinner. In order to achieve speed since 'time is money' the employers keep a very close vigil over them, often scolding or hitting them if they are not working at maximum speed. Some are forced to work with a matchbox placed between their chin and neck in order that they keep their head down obliging them to fully concentrate themselves on their work.

Even forcing children to stay in one place is not unusual as they sit hunched all day over their work. One twelve-year-old girl who earns only five rupees a week recounts to a Human Rights Watch worker the saga of her existence:

> My father and mother forced me to go to work with the agent. The agent often beats me. If I tell my father, he allows me to stay home the following day, but then they are pushing me to go again. My father and mother say I have to go. I don't want to go. I am afraid of my agent. But my parents force me to go, if I don't go, they scold me and beat me.
>
> Every week the agent gives my wages to my parents. If it is less money than usual, they beat me.
>
> In my family there are seven members, so it is difficult to even get enough food to eat. That's why my father goes to the agent—to ask for money. But the agent won't give it, because he says I don't work hard enough. But every day I am being sent back to the agent.[13]

Not only are the children frequently beaten, but they are often subject to chronic pain in their backs, hands and wrists, as well as serious illnesses such as tuberculosis, asthma, and other lung related diseases from which later they often die. Furthermore, even though they only work for a pittance, the girls especially are even cheated out of part of their wages. Furthermore, when they are not cheated the bonded *beedi* rollers are only paid between 20 to 30% of the wages they would be entitled to on the regular, open market. The remaining percentage of their earnings are kept by the agents and are considered interest, thus the annual interest rates are approximately somewhere from 300 to 500%.

Legislation against bonded labor began as early as 1933, when the practice of child debt servitude was made illegal; the Children (Pledging of Labor) Act having been enacted under British rule. Since Independence, another important law was passed in 1976, the Bonded Labor System (Abolition) Act. This law has been considered one of the most significant because

13. Human Rights Watch, *The Small Hands of Slavery*, 46.

not only does it outlaw all bondage, including that of children, but it requires that the government has responsibility for both intervening and rehabilitating the worker. In 1978, the Ministry of Labor initiated a rehabilitation allowance; the Central Government contributing half of the money and the state where the former bonded laborer abided paid the other half. Originally, the allowance was 4,000 rupees and was raised in 1986 to a little over 6,000. Apart from economic aid, the government program included both psychological and physical rehabilitation. This was followed by the Juvenile Justice (Care and Protection) of Children Act of 2000, whereby it was a crime to procure or employ a child in any hazardous employment or in bondage, child bondage becoming punishable by imprisonment. Yet, as can be expected, much of the legislature, whether applying to child labor in general, or more specifically to child bondage, has remained flaunted.

Otherwise, the International Labor Organization (ILO) 1999 Convention No. 182 established an international law which forbade "the worst forms of child labor" including all forms of slavery or practices similar to slavery, whether the sale or trafficking of children, debt bondage and serfdom, and forced or compulsory labor, including forced recruitment of children for use in armed conflict. This law also forbids the use of a child for prostitution, pornography and other illicit activities, such as the trafficking or production of drugs, or other hazardous activities which can be dangerous to them, morally or physically. Although a hundred and fifty-one countries including the United States, signed and domestically ratified this treaty, interestingly India did not; could this be because the government felt it was economically not in their best interest? They equally may have believed that without the income from child labor, many Indian families would fall into a state of total impoverishment and starvation. In some cases, too, when certain activities involving child labor are boycotted, children find themselves in other activities which are more dangerous such as prostitution, street hustling or stone crushing.

In any case, in India, as worldwide, education has been the best weapon against child labor. Yet, under education, India ranks only 124 worldwide, with 63% of the females literate and 81% of the men. Too often in rural India, schools are unavailable, since they are too far away from some of the villages, or the level of schooling is next to non-existent. Furthermore, families are also more often interested in a child's added income than his education. This is particularly true of girls who are destined through marriage to leave the family. This notwithstanding, already in the Constitution, compulsory elementary education was required for all children. Recently, the Right of Children to Free and Compulsory Education Act of 2009 was also passed, mandating free and compulsory education to all children aged six to fourteen. This law also required that 25% of the seats in every private school be allocated for disadvantaged children and physically injured ones.

'Change' agents and various organizations and charities in India are also fighting against child labor, some with better results than others. The 'change' agents work to save children from hazardous labor and oversee that they receive at least the minimal level of primary education. Often, some of these agents also stress the importance of health awareness to both the children and their families. Apart from the 'change' agents, there are also organizations such as Oxfam which fight against child labor. Aware that poverty is at the root of the problem, their efforts are directed at reducing it by funding and directing projects aimed at improving the incomes of disadvantaged families; this, in turn, enables them to educate their children rather than to have them work. This financial assistance also helps to reduce the children's poor health and malnutrition. Otherwise, some charities are also focused on paying the families' debts in order to eliminate child labor. In Tamil Nadu, as an example, charities have helped pay off the family debts so that children working in the matchstick industry can be released from bondage. Yet, unfortunately, more often than not, children are returned once again to a life of slavery. Meanwhile, other agencies and organizations have directed their efforts in reducing the exploitation of child laborers rather than eliminating it entirely.

Child labor in India has been propagated in great part because of the country's unsustainable systems of landholding as well as the caste system in rural areas. Child labor for many Hindus is defendable since each individual is believed to be the product of his *karma*, and the lowest castes along with women and female children are, in particular, the most karmically indebted; their exploitation is thus justifiable. Even at the level of child labor, the rules of patriarchy reign and the girl child is more exploited than her male counterpart. She almost inevitably begins working within the house at an earlier age and once working outside works longer hours and earns less money than a boy for an equivalent job. Child labor, like child marriage, the *devadasi* system and child trafficking and prostitution is a result of intense poverty, lack of education, ignorance and the tenacious grasp of abused religious practices on the society. Finally, India follows the old adage "Laws are only made to be broken". Although the Indian people and their government are becoming constantly more aware of the victimization of millions of Indian children and are thus creating continuous legislation against it, yet, for economical and even psychological and social reasons, enforcement is met with much difficulty since all these practices have been embedded once again in Hindu tradition for centuries.

CHILD TRAFFICKING AND PROSTITUTION

In India, trafficking of minor girls and prostitution is a multi-billion dollar industry; a business that is continually augmenting. Between 2005-06 alone, there was an increase of 60% in the procuration of girls under 18. A majority of them who were and are the victims of trafficking are adolescents between twelve and sixteen years old. Many are bought, sold or kidnapped from the poorer region of India. Otherwise, a large number are brought by traffickers from Bangladesh and particularly Nepal; 100,000 smuggled into the country from Nepal annually.

Today, three million prostitutes work in India's brothels and 40% of them are minors. They are sold by their families to men who pretend to be marriage matchmakers and if not promise them jobs in the cities. They are usually sold because of continued drought, farm debts and unemployment. The middlemen who buy them in turn sell them to pimps, madams and brothel owners. 70% of the prostitutes are illiterate due to their economic situation which denied them almost any education. Furthermore, by the early 2000s about 50% were infected by AIDS and today a majority have contracted the disease, in particular the urban prostitutes who often receive 'the fever' from truck drivers and migrant workers who are traveling far from their families. This is not surprising given that, on an average day, these young prostitutes receive about seven clients, but the number can jump as high as thirty on a very busy day or during the holidays. Yet, one driver proudly recounted to a journalist of the *New Yorker* that he was one of the few that managed to avoid catching AIDS since he simply took a bath with lime and water after having sex. Meanwhile, most prostitutes, themselves, due to their ignorance, refuse to visit a healthcare center since they attach a stigma to such a visit. Otherwise, they have to work off the price paid by the *malik* (brothel owner) or the madam. The customers usually pay a $ 1.10 to $ 2 a sex act, or sometimes a bit more; a fairer girl usually receiving more than a darker one. The madam gets the money up front. However, by the time she deducts for the girl's expenses for food, electricity and rent, and the high interest charges of her purchase price, there is next to nothing left. Consequently, apart from the tips she sometimes receives, these young girls are forced to borrow from money landers at 500% in order to supplant an insufficient diet of rice and dal as well as a few basic expenditures; thus, they are constantly in debt. Additionally, they are systematically harassed by the police and even though the madam pays the police weekly bribes in order to protect herself, each girl services several police gratuitously.

Since 1986, the age of girls entering prostitution has been declining. In 1998, the average age of girls was eighteen. By 2000, it was fifteen, and three years later, girls as young as twelve were readily available. Now clients are asking for them as young as eight. Unfortunately, their ages have continually decreased and in some very exceptional cases girls as young as five or even three have been forced into prostitution with the help of the Internet. With the problem of contagious diseases and particularly AIDS, some clients, particularly those from the Arab countries, place an enormous premium on a girl's virginity. At the sex auctions where the affluent Arabs from the Persian Gulf bid against opulent Indian men, a nine-year-old virgin can bring in as much as 60,000 rupees, approximately $ 2,000. Additionally, Indian men are particularly superstitious when it comes to sex. They believe that having sexual intercourse with a virgin will make them invulnerable to disease and can even cure syphilis and gonorrhea. Others also believe that having sex with boys will make them more potent, while still others are convinced sex with a virgin will reduce the possibility of becoming infected by sexually transmitted disease.

Mumbai is deemed 'Asia's largest sex bazaar'. The city's prostitution is an efficacious business which is under the control of four criminal groups. The first governs the police bribes, the second controls moneylending, the third sustains the district's internal laws and order, the fourth, which is viewed as the most important, supervises the procurement of girl children and women in an enormous network stretching between South India to the Himalayas in the North. Mumbai, itself, has two major red-light districts, Falkland Road and Kamathipura, appropriately named the 'place of pleasure'. They are two connected areas in the south-central part of the city which are sandwiched together between boundless Hindu and Muslim slums. Falkland Road is well located with two nearby railway stations and twenty-five lanes of wooden brothels with gilded balconies scattered among small restaurants, car repair shops, liquor stores, two hundred bars, flophouses, immense tenements and three police stations, which are mainly symbolic at best. There is also a school, which is also emblematic since only 5% of the students ever graduate. Falkland Road is located at the center of Mumbai's red-light district in an area appropriately called 'the Cages' as the prostitutes are displayed in windows and in 4-by-6 foot *pinjaras* (cages); the most desirable, meaning the youngest and best looking are displayed where they are the most visible. When they are not relegated like animals to their cages, a dozen of them are squeezed together like sardines in a 10×10 room in very unhygienic conditions. The rooms in the brothels are usually full of movie idols and sometimes ironically even religious icons. Eunuch Lane is another center of attraction along Falkland Road. There are approximately 2,000 *hijras* (eunuchs). These transvestites are renowned for their beauty and are extremely feminine dressed in saris or black leather skirts; they cater mainly to the Sikhs. While the sex workers on Falkland Rd. work day and night, the flesh trade in Kamathipura brothels is restricted to nighttime. Kamathipura was established during the late seventeenth century to satisfy the British troops. It is a small rectangle of fourteen lanes, roughly three blocks wide and very accessible to Grant Road train station. There are residential buildings, tea shops, pharmacies and convenience stores scattered among the *pinjara* and the brothels.

Prostitution here can be divided into three groups: slavery and debt bondage, *adhiya* and lodgers. Victims of sex trafficking are initially held in a form of slavery or debt-bondage. The *adhiya*, which means 'one-half' system are those who remain in the brothel and divide their earnings with the *malik*, the brothel owner and often collaborate with the *gharwalis* (madams) in adapting the new slaves to the brutality of the brothel. The lodgers are actually renters; even though they no longer live on the premises, they rent rooms in order to serve their clients, they usually only charge their customers around $ 1.10 for sex because they are in their thirties and thus older than the others.

In Mumbai's red-light district most are slaves and those in debt-bondage. The trafficker who acts as the agent or middleman often earns 5,000 rupees for placing young boys in bonded labor and as much as 200,000 rupees, $ 3,000 for girls sold for prostitution or child marriage. The girls after having been bought or kidnapped and brought to the brothel, spend a few very arduous weeks where they are indoctrinated into their new existence. They are locked away in dungeons, sometimes even with snakes, and given next to nothing to either drink or eat. They are also tortured, beaten and raped daily in order to break their will and make them more submissive, a quality required by their clients. Should they show any form of discontent with their lot, they are immediately whipped. These girls usually never remain in one brothel but are often shifted from place to place in order to avoid police detection. Their procurer renames them and insists that they never reveal anything personal about themselves such as their original name or address. Apart from discretion, they are taught to treat their clients with a maximum amount of courtesy. The brothels where they are kept have two entries so in case of a raid, they can escape. Due to violence, malnutrition, disease, or lack of medical cure, it is not surprising that most never reach forty. Those who are rescued from prostitution are faced with the dilemma that their families consider them a disgrace and will rarely take them back.

In Mumbai, 15% of the prostitutes are *devadasis* and about 50% are Nepalis. In many of the Mumbai brothels, one or two floors are even dedicated to the girls from Nepal. They have particular appeal due to their fair skin, slender bodies and Asian features. They are demurer than the Indian girls and do not try and hustle their customers for money. They are also shyer, since they speak next to no Hindi. In a word, they are more manageable. Their presence has, in fact, created a problem with the Nepalis Government. In a SAARC conference held in the mid-nineties on the girl child, the Nepalis manifested great anger toward the Indians for permitting the trafficking of their girls for prostitution in the Indian brothels in Delhi and Mumbai. Likewise, the Bangladesh equally contested the trafficking and sale of their girls to Sonagachi, the red-light district in Kolkata. Yet, many of the prostitutes, whether Indian or Nepalis are tortured, drugged and some even murdered as described by one of the girls who was working in Mumbai's red-light district:

> Minors are starved and beaten when they first arrive. The *gharwali* gives them opium so they will have sex. If they do not behave, the *malik* makes the radio high and beats them until they go unconscious. Just a few days back a minor came from my village and was sold

> by her parents for twenty thousand rupees ($ 444). She refused to have sex, so the *malik* broke her arm.[14]

Another prostitute addresses the problem of AIDS and the consequences for the next generation:

> For twenty-one years I have been at Falkland Road. I was too young when I was sold to this work, I did not know any better. I only do it now because I have no choice. Now that I have HIV, I do not know how much longer I will live. Who will protect my daughter when I am gone?[15]

Prerana is a reputed anti-trafficking organization in Mumbai founded by Priti Patkar in 1986. Prerana brought together a group of organizations to confront the problem of trafficking in minors; the group formed the network Against Commercial Sexual Exploitation and Trafficking aimed at working with women within the red-light district. Today, Prerana has about 250 members who work in areas where girls are trafficked throughout the state. Patkar has established three emergency shelters clandestinely placed throughout the city. They are open twenty-four hours a day and house the daughters of prostitutes in order to avoid that they do not follow in their mothers' footsteps. Some are the orphans of mothers who have died of AIDS, while others are the children of prostitutes who are alive. Otherwise, almost inevitably daughters in their turn also become prostitutes and sons, pimps. Since its establishment in 1986, Prerana focuses on terminating intergenerational prostitution and protecting women and children from child trafficking by promoting their education and health. The organization has supported victims from prevention to repatriation.

One of the shelters, the Naunihal Special Home for Girls, housing girls from eight to twenty, was visited by the notorious Hollywood fitness trainer, Ramona Braganza. Completely intrigued by the girls, she began a fitness program for them and now a group of them have become gainfully employed as fitness trainers in Mumbai.

14. Siddharta Kara, *Sex Trafficking: Inside the Business of Modern Slavery* (N.Y.: Columbia University Press, 2009), 49-50.
15. *Ibid.*, 50.

Jubilee Action is another organization in Mumbai directed also at rescuing the daughters of prostitutes. It has two houses located on the outskirts of the city and provides permanent homes for the adopted and orphaned children of prostitutes working along Falkland Road or in Kamathipura. Some fifty girls have been rescued by the staff and others have been brought by their mothers in order to spare them the dangers of the street. The girls are sent to the local schools and given their lack of formal education also receive additional tutoring.

Ladies clubs also exist and are associated with a milder and more sophisticated form of prostitution which is unique to Mumbai. Women, usually after saying a prayer, sing and dance for wealthy male spectators who excitedly throw cash to them from their seats. Even though they are not allowed to solicit the women while on the premises of the club, it is permitted that they take their phone numbers and meet them outside. There is a very ritualistic aspect to this spectacle and one which is well described by Somini Sengupta in the *New York Times*:

> A dozen women in shimmering chiffon skirts swayed their hip, lip-synched and gazed at themselves in the mirrored walls...in one corner of the bar, a man kept his attention and his money focused on a languid young girl in yellow. She moved to the music, threw back her hair, admired herself in the mirror and responded to his invitations to move closer, each time fattening the stack of bills in her hand.[16]

Meanwhile, in 2005 the ladies bars were at risk of being closed down because some Mumbai officials connected to the Hindu nationalist group, Shiv Sena, deemed that the dancing clubs were promoting prostitution and endangering family life.

The *mujra* or clandestine courtesan clubs are similar and are particularly well known in Lahore. The dancers do not perform a strip tease act but dance lewdly shaking their breasts and their bottoms, wearing bells around their ankles. Maureen Paton wrote in the *Times of London* that women:

---

16. Somini Sengupta, "Live Clothed Girls may be Stripped of their Dance Jobs", *New York Times Asia Pacific*, 2 May, 2005, 4.

> Wearing leather ankle straps hung with bells below their traditional costumes of tunic and leggings, will simply mime to film music. As a signal to show his appreciation, a man will toss a £ 5 or £ 10 note in the direction of the chosen girl. And after the performance is over, sexual services are bought and sold in an adjoining room. Nothing needs to be spelled out: it is understood that sex, if the client wishes, is part of the equation.[17]

Kolkata is another city renown for prostitution, having one of the largest industries within the country. The largest red-light district is Sonagachi which employs nine thousand of the twenty thousand prostitutes working in the city. The brothel landlords, pimps and madams who operate the three hundred and sixty-two brothels are also influent within Kolkata. There are as many forty thousand clients visiting there districts daily and as in the other urban red-light districts, they are frequented predominantly by a wealthy clientele, consisting of businessmen, members of the film and advertising industries, diamond merchants and politicians. The prostitutes, themselves, in Kolkata have created union-like organizations, the Durbar Mahila Samanwaya Committee (DMSC) or Committee on the Coordination of Unstoppable Women and are united to fight for their rights. Among the diverse groups, one of them is primarily focused on having the prostitutes' customers practice safe sex and systematically use condoms. This particular group has also assisted the girls and women protect themselves from the constant harassment created by gangsters and police raids. They have also focused on the education of the sex workers, so that they might be eligible for another form of job. Simultaneously, they are actively advocating that prostitution be made legal so that these workers will share the same rights as others who make their living in different areas.

Another important way which child trafficking and prostitution are being addressed is through public art. Kolkata-based photographer and installation artist, Leena Kejriwal, has begun a public art project, "Missing". Leena and volunteers

---

17. Maureen Paton, "Playing Away: The Asian Sex Trade", *Times of London*, 23 March 2005, 4 (s).

are stenciling walls and other public areas across the country with life-size silhouettes of young girls. The purpose is to create awareness of the number of girls kidnapped or lured away from their homes, schools and workplaces by traffickers who sell them into the flesh industry. Her project began in January 2014 when she created a four-and-a-half meter-tall iron and fiberglass installation of missing girls for the India Art Fair, one of the country's most visited exhibitions in New Delhi. Most Indians were completely unaware of the situation and have responded very favorably to her undertaking. In 2015 in order to extend these figures to other cities, Kejriwal crowd-funded more than 1.6 million rupees ($ 24,000) through Wishberry in June and July 2015.

New Delhi, the nation's capital has its red-light district along Garstin Bastion Road. Ironically, Delhi, considered India's most important city, seems to be the home of less prostitution than either Mumbai or even Kolkata. During the day, GB Road houses a large hardware market but by night becomes Delhi's center for prostitution. Roughly, three thousand five hundred women and their children live in ninety degenerate brothels. Of these prostitutes, 50% are *devadasis*. The hardware stores close at night but the dark staircases are overflowing with the queues of clients waiting to be serviced. There are sometimes pimps at the doorways selling their produce: "Young girl, *Bhai* (bro). Pretty. Price good, price good". The largest brothel, Kotha 64, is halfway down the road. In the first room, the windows are boarded up; the floors are filled with refuse, mainly used condoms and cigarette butts. There are LED lights and around the sides of the room there are a dozen, really minute compartments where the girls await their clients.

In Delhi, itself, there are small charities, as the NGO Kat Katha which provides schooling for some of the children as well as medical check-ups for their mothers. However, these organizations are constantly combatting financial problems as well as ongoing threats from the underworld.

Otherwise, there is also much prostitution and child trafficking in communities outside the large cities. In the past not only was dance associated with prostitution but also music and theatre as well as entertainment in general. Entertainers traditionally were issue of the entertainment castes who were and are still ranked at a low level in the caste and purity system. Female folk entertainers are known for frequently prostituting themselves. Galandars, for example, are acrobats, bear handlers, jugglers, magicians and impersonators who travel from one place to another. Sometimes the women entertainers exchange their favors for camping possibilities or grazing rights. The Kangar, for instance, are a group of such artisans, entertainers, singers, dancers, musicians, carnival operators and now prostitutes who are widely known throughout South and Southeast Asia.

Otherwise, the Bedia, a tribal community which resides along the Jaipur Highway outside Bharatpur were also historically entertainers in Rajasthan and Madhya, the women and girls performing for the feudal lords. Now, their family business has become prostitution, a profession in which they take great pride. Adolescent girls become prostitutes while their brothers become agents. Apart from the Kangars and the Bedia, there are also tribal communities who now make their living also by commercial sex; the Nuts and Sanshis being an example.

Another source of potential child prostitutes is the Sunderban region; it is the world's largest swamp forest in the estuary of the Ganges. It is located on a delta near the Bay of Bengal and consists of fifty-four small islands. Several villages are alluded to as 'Widows' villages because many of the men die as a consequence of their hazardous professions such as deep-sea fishing, or prawn seed or forest produce collection. Many are devoured alive or crippled by crocodiles or other dangerous wild animals. Middlemen from the brothels seek young girls from female headed families who thus are financially in need of aid. In this case, they are neither kidnapped nor abducted, but leave voluntarily. They take these girls usually of ages thirteen or fourteen to the Sonagachi red-light area of Kolkata where they often work as long as ten years sending money back to their families.

Child prostitution which is much more a female occurrence, still also exists among young boys. It is particularly well known among the launda dancers or dancing boys, who are once again members of the entertainment castes. These young gender variant boys have a very feminine demeanor and are consequently the victims of a social stigma to such an extent that it is next to impossible for them to find work in any mainstream profession. Consequently, many integrate themselves into the *hijra* (eunuch) community and undergo very dangerous surgery which is also illegal. Only 50% of these boys who are operated on by a *Dai*, quacks and doctors of a dubious reputation manage to survive. The launda dancers are mainly from very poor families in West Bengal, who they help support. They usually migrate to Uttar Pradesh and Bihar during the wedding seasons in the spring and fall. They frequently remain for several months at a time and are contracted by wedding orchestras where almost inevitably these young boys are exploited financially and sexually. 90% describe their first sexual experience between the age of nine and twelve and one which was forced upon them. During the wedding festivals, dressed as women, performing for the poorer families since the wealthier ones use instead female dancers, they lead the groom's entourage to the bride's home and are thus a focal point of the ceremony. At this time, they are exposed to a largely male group. Sexual abuse is renown to occur after these processions late at night. Often, they are burnt with cigarettes, bitten, assaulted and gang raped at knifepoint, frequently being mutilated with knife blades before being raped. Those who protest are often killed.

Meanwhile, in India, Bangalore is the third largest city after Delhi and Mumbai, and is also well known for prostitution among boys. Young boys first become sex workers, again by force, between the ages of ten and thirteen. They come from poor, illiterate families and usually earn 5,000 rupees, $ 106 nightly, more than they could ever dream of earning in a regular job. Jagruth, a non-governmental organization that aids these prostitutes has created a medical clinic with the goal of educating the boys about the prevention dangers of HIV/AIDS but is fighting an upstream battle because it lacks the support of both the community and the government. Otherwise, although some boys are aware of the perils of STDs such as HIV/AIDS, few ever use condoms because they are under the illusion that their well-dressed clients are inevitably free of any disease.

Lastly, monsoon-ravaged villages, as well as railway stations are also particularly propitious locations for traffickers. They collect the orphans or buy the children of farmers who have become destitute after the monsoon. Meanwhile, Bangalore's railway station with eighty trains arriving daily is one of the most notorious places for traffickers to find runaway children, usually fleeing poverty or their parents' brutality; most runaways are boys because girls are often already sold by their families. The trafficking became so rampant there that a Catholic priest, Father George, launched an organization, Bosco, which provides shelter and schooling for the runaways who do not return to their families. Of the fifty to sixty children arriving daily, Father George considers his organization fortunate if it can save fifteen. Bosco has seven homes and one hundred staff members who work in the day, others at night. Rainbow House is one of the shelters run by Bosco. Fifty-six girls live in two empty rooms with no chairs or tables. They play, sleep and do their homework on the floor and all eat together in the hallway. They all came from very disadvantaged families and in some cases, this is the first home they ever had. Apart from their studies, the children also need to be socialized and are taught very basic behavior such as the importance of cleanliness or not hitting other children when a disagreement occurs.

Anti-sex trafficking activist Ruchira Gupta has played a major role in combatting the sex trafficking industry in India. Gupta founded Apne Aap Women Worldwide, a grassroots organization to assist at risk girls and women. She founded Apne Aap with twenty-three former prostitutes who protected her when she was in the midst of filming a Mumbai brothel and a criminal held a knife to her and menaced to slit her throat. The girls crowded around Gupta and told her potential slayer that if he was to kill her, he would have to kill all them. The organization now has twenty thousand members and has thus far sent sixty-six traffickers to prison. Its goals are education, a respectable livelihood, legal protection, and safe and independent living facilities. The organization takes children out of red-light areas and places them in schools and community learning centers. It furthermore helps to train prostitutes for a more dignified employment and provides them with a monetary savings. It additionally assists them to take advantage of the government's "below poverty housing" and it has also created centers to give the prostitutes legal aid in understanding their rights while explaining the deleterious effect of sex trafficking throughout the world. Gupta furthermore insists that pornography has played a most insidious role in sex trafficking of young girls. The habitual programs whether on TV or in films involves sex with pain and violence for girls and women. The media at all levels including, of course, the magazines and the newspapers whether deliberately or not are considered contributors in the rise of child prostitution and trafficking. Finally, even though the original founders of Apne Aap have now all died of AIDS, hunger, or suicide, Gupta still hopes to continue her work beyond Mumbai, Bihar, Delhi and West Bengal where her organization works in local communities; her next target is the U.S. where the problem is widespread.

Furthermore, Kailash Satyarthi who was awarded the Nobel Prize in 2014 with Malala Yousafzai of Pakistan, saved the lives of eighty thousand children from labor and prostitution through his organization Bachpan Bachao Andolan (Save the Childhood Movement). He lauds Modi for his 2016 move to curb 'black money' by withdrawing overnight the 500 and 1,000 rupee notes in order to reduce corruption and counterfeit currency. Satyarthi who is a children's rights and education advocate believes that Modi's unexpected initiative has greatly assisted in reducing child trafficking, prostitution and slavery.

Meanwhile, legislation has been passed in order to combat child prostitution and trafficking. In 1956, India passed the Suppression of Immoral Traffic in Women and Girls Act. As it proved to be inadequate, Parliament amended the law in 1970 and later in 1986. The law aimed to inhibit and better yet abolish commercialized sexual abuse and exploitation and traffic in persons as an organized livelihood. The purpose of this law was not only to punish those who were guilty, but also to rescue and rehabilitate the victims. During 2004 and 2005, police closed down twenty-one brothels where minors were working. The Immoral Traffic (Prevention) Act and certain provisions of the Indian Penal Code punishes offenders by sealing the premises of the establishment for a maximum period of three years. The accused is also subject to punishment for a minimum of ten years. Even though the laws have had some effect, it has been noted that generally the police and the politicians have had relatively little success in enforcing many of them; this is due in part to incapacity and otherwise to unwillingness. Bribery, at one level or another, is also very frequent and the border guards between India and Nepal are notorious for allowing traffickers to slip by after large handouts. Although between 1997 and 2000, seventy suspected traffickers with two hundred and seventy girls were caught, in 2014 as an example, there were only a hundred convictions for offenders in child prostitution and trafficking. However, 2016 was a landmark year because India's ministry prepared a new anti-trafficking law which modernized many outdated laws such as, and amazingly, treating the victims as the criminals instead of their offenders, but the bill is yet to be implemented. Otherwise, and as is so frequently the case, laws are too frequently not enforced, and their existence alone seems too often to be adequate contentation.

After the arms sale, trafficking of persons is the second largest trade in the world. Every day, about two hundred thousand girls and women in India become prostitutes, 80% against their will. Every hour four girls and women enter prostitution, three of whom are forced into the trade, almost inevitably as a result of trafficking. It is estimated given the current rate of growth that by 2025, one out of five Indian girls are destined to the flesh trade. After Thailand, India has the largest number of child prostitutes. While poverty is the dominant reason, other factors such as well-organized crime rings, insufficient law enforcement, and the dissolution of the family combined with the girl's generally inferior status are contributing components. While child marriage, the *devadasi* system, and child labor on the whole are on the decline, the trafficking and prostitution of young girls is unquestionably on the rise.

The position of women and especially the ex-Untouchable ones was well summarized in a speech by Nehru in Allahabad in 1928, when he stated that "the future of India cannot consist of dolls and playthings and if you made half the population of the country a mere plaything of the other half, an encumbrance on others, how will you ever make progress? Therefore, I say that you must face the problem boldly and attack the roots of the evil."[18] The malevolence, however, goes back centuries and is rooted in the *Manusmriti*, the *Bhagavad Gita* and the *Ramayana*, all of whom sanctified the enslavement of Indian women. Women's status in India is entrenched in religion and tradition and women's enlightenment is necessary to uplift them from male patriarchal bondage. With the Constitution and the Hindu Code Bill and the consequent increased educational possibilities and economic independence, they are beginning to transcend the status of dolls and 'playthings'. Currently, India's laws protecting women and children, particularly girls, must not only be ratified, but must be urgently enforced to safeguard them as well as Indian society at large. Unfortunately, the female of all ages must constantly combat the dictates of Manu, while in China, but to a lesser extent, she is similarly struggling against the patriarchal and disrespectful voice of Confucianism.

---

18. Jagat Bright, MA. ed., *Important Speeches of Jawaharlal Nehru: A Collection of Most Significant Speeches Delivered by Jawaharlal Nehru from 1922-45* (Lahore: The Indian Printing Works, 1945), 69.

Chapter 2

Adoption of Children in India: The Hidden Reality

In India, initially adoption played a significant role as early as Hindu mythology. The stories of Krishna, Karna, Andal, Sita as well as many others are demonstrative of the consequential relationship between the adoptee and adoptive parents. Today, India which has remained overwhelmingly patriarchal has still been plagued by female feticide, infanticide, and abandonment and the baby girl, when not aborted or killed has now become the central focus of local and international adoption. Like China during the peak of its One-child policy, and seemingly even worse, these infants are too often the victims of laundering not only within the country but particularly in inter-country adoption where the financial stakes are high. Both the sending and the receiving countries conveniently remain most of the time in denial, a state which best suits their economic interests. E.J. Graff in her article, "The Lie We Love", has well resumed the current situation: "Foreign adoption seems like the perfect solution to a heartbreaking imbalance: poor countries have babies in need of homes, and rich countries have homes in need of babies. Unfortunately, those little orphaned bundles of joy may not be orphans at all."[1]

By the end of the last century female infanticide became rampant in some parts of India. In Jaisalmer, India's some communities have lowest sex ratio. Throughout the country, when a child is not killed through deliberate neglect, the common ways of killing girls have been *dudhapiti*, applying opium to

1. E.J. Graff, "The Lie We Love", *Foreign Policy* (November/December 2008), 59.

the mother's nipple and then feeding the baby, suffocating her with a rug, feeding her poisonous oleander berries, or simply dedicating her to a goddess. Baby girls are also fed poisonous milk of 'irukkan' and 'kalli' plants or crude husks of rice are simply dropped into the baby's throat. However, as police have become more active in fighting infanticide, parents are resorting to what they consider 'more gruesome' but 'less evident' means of suffocating their baby girls in order to avoid post-mortem problems with the authorities. Now, for instance, one of the more innovative ways of asphyxiating a newborn is by feeding her very hot, spicy soup. After a few hours of squirming and screaming, she dies.

The rise of female infanticide in Tamil Nadu reached such proportions that in 1992 baby cradles were placed throughout the state in order to avoid abandonment, and particularly to discourage infanticide. Although never to the extent of Jaisalmer, Tamil Nadu has had one of the highest rates of infanticide in the country. In fact, even during British rule, the English reported many cases a century earlier. Meanwhile, the cradles are the equivalent of China's baby hatches. They are attached to welfare centers, hospitals, police stations, temples and government offices. Once a baby is placed in the cradle, a bell rings three minutes later informing the staff that a child has been deposited. The child will then be left with a child welfare committee. A panel further examines the baby in order to decide whether child is in a condition, physically and mentally, to be adopted. The main reason for abandonment is because the baby, usually deserted in the first week is a girl, and she will require a dowry which will eat up as much as two-thirds of a family's assets. Boys on the other hand, like in China, have both social, economic and religious advantages. They carry on the family lineage, they can support financially the family and take care of their parents in old age, and they light the family members' funeral pyre which allows them the possibility of salvation. The second motivation for abandonment is simply poverty.

Abandonment of baby girls in India is also reminiscent of China during the apex of the One-child policy. However, desertion today in China is predominantly due to physical or mental illness of the child, demonstrating that India remains more embedded in the patriarchal system. Interestingly, too, Indians accept infanticide much more easily than abandonment; maybe that is why laws exist against fœticide and abandonment, but not against infanticide. Among the villagers there is a popular Tamil saying, "we may give children to Yama (the Hindu God of death) but none to others (in adoption)". Additionally, abandoning threatens a man's image as a provider and protector as reflected in statements such as the following: "He (household head) cannot bring up a daughter, is he a man?".[2] One of the local mothers also claimed:

> Only mothers who have got a child in wrong ways will surrender. A true mother will never have the heart to do so. She will say, "if the baby is killed, I will be upset for two days". But this is better than thinking "Am I a mother? I gave away my offspring."[3]

This shameless, matter of fact attitude toward infanticide found also in rural China is furthermore reflected when a female is faced with keeping a baby girl or boy. One pregnant woman claimed very pragmatically:

> if it's a boy, I'll keep him, but I'm very poor. If it's a girl, I'll kill her.[4]

In India, like in China, it is illegal to abandon a child. In the Indian Constitution, it is not legal to desert or neglect a child. By Section 317 of the Indian Penal Code, parents can be incarcerated up to seven years or fined. Similarly, they can receive a prison term of three years and/or fine under Section 25 of the Juvenile Justice Act, of 2015. However, like the baby hatches, parents in India, too, who anonymously surrender a child to a cradle are exempt from punishment. In fact, similar to the baby hatches, the cradles are a subject of controversy. Some

2. Sharada Srinivasan and Anju S. Bedi, "Daughter Elimination: Cradle Baby Scheme in Tamil Nadu", *Economic & Political Weekly*, LXV, No. 23 (June 5, 2010), 20.
3. Srinivasan and Bedi, "Daughter Elimination: Cradle Baby Scheme in Tamil Nadu", 20.
4. Emily Buchanan, *From China With Love: A Long Road to Motherhood* (West Sussex, England: John Wiley & Sons, 2005), 71.

opine that they are an encouragement for abandoning children to government care and a means of absolving parents of their responsibility. Others believe that the cradles act as a means whereby a child can avoid infanticide or abandonment in such places such as dumpsters, ditches, bus stations, train tracks, lakes and rivers, often placed in plastic bags or wrapped in threadbare blankets, where few will have the chance of survival.

Thus, also in 1992, in Tamil Nadu, the government created the Girl Child Protection Scheme (GCPS) which provides financial incentives to families having only daughters and no sons and where one of the parents has undergone sterilization before the age of thirty-five. The plan is intended to eradicate female fœticide, infanticide and abandonment, and promote the welfare and status of girls who are issue of poor families. As females, are perceived as an economic burden, the plan is a means of enhancing their economic value by helping families to support them. This is done by depositing a certain sum of money in an interest-bearing security which is used to make payments to the various households below the poverty line on a regular basis. In Tamil Nadu, there has been a decreasing number of abandoned cradle babies and the CSR has also improved from 826 in 2001 to 911 in 2011. Similar schemes have also been implemented throughout the country such as Dikri Bachao campaign of Gujarat, the Devi Rupak Scheme of Haryana, the Ladli campaign of Delhi and the scheme for cash incentives to *panchayats*[5] for improving the village sex ratio of Punjab. Cradles have now also been placed throughout India in the hopes that female infanticide and abandonment will continue to decrease. In order to reach these goals as well as an improved CSR, it is necessary to stringently enforce the Dowry Prohibition Act of 1961 and the PCPNDT (Pre-Conception and Pre-Natal Diagnostic Techniques) Act of 1994 as well as to pass the Women Reservation Bill to ensure 33% of the members of the Parliament are female.

Until recently, adoption in India has largely been thwarted by religion. Hinduism is constantly present even in adoption.

5. Local assemblies.

Although informal adoption within family and extended family has existed for centuries, always, of course, motivated by the necessity of an heir for religious and secular purposes, stranger adoption was only legalized after Independence in 1956 by the Hindu Adoption and Maintenance Act (HAMA). However, the Act was only limited to Hindus, Buddhists, Jains, or Sikhs. Some of the more pertinent conditions were the following: both married and singles can adopt, if a biological child exists in the family a child of the opposite sex has to be adopted, children adopted under this act get the same legal rights as a biological child, children under fifteen can be adopted, a single man adopting a girl should be at least twenty-one years older than the child and likewise a single woman adopting a boy should be at least twenty-one years older than the child. Importantly, a Hindu could adopt a daughter as well as an orphan (a child of unknown parentage) which was not possible before. A widow, spinster, single, or a divorced woman could now also adopt which was also not feasible prior to this law. Another important ramification was that adoption could occur only with the consent of the wife. Finally, all these conditions are irrevocable.

The non-Hindus, meaning the Muslims, Christians, Jews, and the Parsis were not covered under HAMA and their Personal Laws did not sanction adoption. Thus, there remained no possibility to adopt and their only alternative was to take a child as their ward under the Guardians and Wards Act of 1890, a law which was passed under the British rule of India when there was a preoccupation to find guardians who had to take care of destitute orphans. However, the same rights as a biological child were not inherent for the ward and the guardianship ended when the child reached eighteen; the ward finding himself completely unprotected.

In fact, it was not until 2006 with the Amendment Act of the Juvenile Justice (Care and Protection) Act of 2000, that any Indian citizen could adopt a child who is legally free for adoption, that the religion of the adoptive parent or parents is irrelevant, and among other stipulations that the adoptee had the same legal rights as the biological child. In other words, it was not until recently that roughly 15% of the Indian population had the right to adopt a child, at all.

Most of the destitute and unwanted children are born to young, unmarried women under twenty-five who abandon their offspring due to a poor economic situation. These unwed mothers, furthermore, wish to avoid social stigma and do not in any way wish to jeopardize their marriage possibilities. Simultaneously, most of the adoptive parents are married between thirty and forty. The Hindu parents particularly living in India are usually more traditional and demanding in their selection of an adopted child. They usually request a very young child (below six months), a light-skinned male definitely without any tribal features, often of a similar caste and religion, when known. Strangely, for some the child's horoscope can be even more important than either caste or religion, as it is perceived as a means of determining compatibility. Those Indians living abroad, foreigners and/or individuals of other religions tend to be more flexible. Not only do they often favor girls, but even adopt older children, siblings and those with special needs. Otherwise, those who have adopted under HAMA tend to be slightly older, less educated, of a lower socio-economic group and significantly the couple has been married for a longer period of time, some waiting as long as fifteen, even twenty years before taking the plunge to adopt. This factor is almost inevitably linked to the difficulty faced by them in front of their infertility which is still a complex problem, particularly in traditional India.

Infertility, which is a great problem in China seems to take on even worse proportions particularly in rural India. Some women even parade for months with a pillow around their stomach and when normally they should deliver, they enter a hospital and sometimes a friend or the adoption agency secretly brings them a child which they pretend to family and society is their own. However, this has become more complicated because the new Supreme Court guidelines do not allow licensed agencies to give a child in adoption before it is declared legally free for adoption either by the juvenile justice system or after the sixty-day waiting period in the case that a child has been relinquished by its parents. Therefore, it becomes impossible to pretend that the child is a newborn.

Otherwise, in India, barrenness is a curse and a barren woman is known as a *banjh* a *banjhni*, or a *sookhi kokh*. The childless woman is even harassed, beaten and her husband often threatens her with desertion. She is furthermore deemed inauspicious. It is considered unlucky to see her not only early in the morning or while going out to the fields for sowing or to another village, but also at rituals such as childbirth, weddings and marriages. Infertility is always blamed on the women and men rarely agree to undergo any fecundity tests. Apart from being treated physically by a *Dai*, she often resorts for a *kohl bharapia* or *bandobast*, to the supernatural consulting of a female/male healer who claims to be possessed by a god or goddess in order to assist in a pregnancy. She usually also visits shrines, does *parikarmas* (circumambulations) around temples, and participates in *pujas* and other religious ceremonies to help the arrival of the long-awaited child, preferably a son, since, furthermore, parents who do not have a son are called '*aputraka*'. They are given a low social status and they, themselves, feel cursed. The male child is seen as '*swogati*' and important for carrying on the family lineage, while the daughter becomes '*parogotri*' on marriage. Despite her uselessness, a daughter is still always preferable to infertility. Otherwise, when the less conventional methods for treating infertility fail, with her family's consent, the wife also consults a traditional doctor.

Meanwhile, Minister for Women and Child Development, Maneka Gandhi, as well as others involved in adoption are extremely preoccupied with the decreasing number of in-country adoptions in India which have diminished by 47% in the last six years. According to CARA, the Central Adoption Resource Agency, the in-country adoptions were 5,693 in 2010 and had fallen to 3,011 in 2015-16. Although the difference was less significant, the inter-country adoptions also dropped during this period from 628 in 2010 to 578 in 2016. Maharashtra has had the highest adoption record. Afterwards, the South Indian states such as Kerala, Karnataka, Tamil Nadu, Andhra Pradesh have maintained a relatively high rate of adoption in comparison to states such as Bihar, Jharkhand, Goa and Uttarakhand as well as the North Eastern states which have reported a drastically low number of adoptions; the abysmally low statistics in these regions are attributed to the lack of adoption agencies. Gandhi has proposed a form of competition between the various adoption agencies who will be rated between platinum to gold, reminiscent of the silver and gold frequent flyer cards. The agencies are to be classified according to the number of adoptions which are carried out and the speed in which they are performed, including how quickly they obtain the necessary court orders. The performing agencies are awarded cash prizes for their achievements, while the non-performing ones eliminate themselves entirely.

Although India is a country, unlike the United States, that has absolutely no history of stranger adoption which accounts in part for the low adoption rate, however it does not justify the recent decrease in adoption within the country and also internationally. Unfortunately, this can be attributed predominantly to child trafficking. The problem of child trafficking first gained much attention in 1982. The practice of placing children abroad for adoption became extremely controversial when an Indian child died in transit to an adoptive home abroad. Simultaneously, based on a newspaper report, an advocate who was in touch with one of the judges of the Supreme Court, claimed that escorts were bringing Indian children to the United States and selling them for $ 2,000 each. He claimed that voluntary agencies were involved in malpractice, leading to the creation of CARA. Today, many Indians, even though they may have to pay more, often prefer to avoid the endless wait and bureaucratic problems involved in traditional adoption. Many infants, the exact number of which is completely unknown, are being bought directly from traffickers, unorthodox orphanage deals or illegally through doctors, nurses, midwives, hospitals, and nursing homes. This is certainly facilitated by the fact that there are no laws against illegal adoption. There are also hair-raising tales of some women who give birth to a normal baby which is replaced with a dead one, telling the mother that her child is stillborn. The healthy child is then trafficked, and the dead baby is taken to the river for burial by the alleged parents. One of the more recent adoption scandals involved a gang of eighteen who stole babies from nursing homes smuggling them out in biscuit boxes, and keeping them at adoptive centers before selling them to Indian and foreign couples. Today, in this illegal market a healthy infant girl is often worth 100 rupees, while the equivalent boy is worth the double. This notwithstanding, adoption agencies report that with the exception of the very orthodox and traditional Hindus, families are now looking to adopt girls more than boys. This is certainly due in great part to all the favorable publicity and the financial incentives given to parents with girl children. Some guilt is probably also involved; adopting a girl child is also a form of compensation for all the injustices they have suffered. Apart from these factors, many believe that daughters are more caring and more attached, while they are afraid that boys could be more problematic at a later age when they learn of their adoption. Finally, as there are many more girls who are up for adoption, the adoption procedure for a girl takes roughly six months, while for a boy can take anywhere from two to four years. In any case, even though parents usually choose the first child, they are shown up to six children.

Apart from trafficking, the adoptive agencies have also acted as a deterrent in many adoptions. Gandhi has in fact been very critical of the "idleness and deliberate lying"[6] of the agencies. Generally, by the Hague Convention, children should first be placed locally, however, the agencies tend whenever possible to place them in foreign adoption because it is much more lucrative. While CARA has capped local adoption at 46,000 rupees, and foreign adoption at $ 5,000, these limits, however, are rarely respected. Foreign parents are even forced to pay as much as $ 35,000 to $ 40,000 to private adoption agencies that act as middlemen. Similarly, donations are also forbidden, but are still solicited by many of the agencies, some asking as much as 150,000 rupees, claiming that since they are not

6. Vishakh Unnikrishnan, "Delhi UC slams Central Adoption Agency, blames it for low adoption rates", 20 July 2016, CatchNews, www.catchnews.com/india-news/

government subsidized, they need some outside funding in order to survive.

Since online adoption began in 2015, the adoption system in India has become much more transparent and efficacious. Furthermore, prospective parents can now adopt anywhere in India as they are no longer obliged to reside for a period of time where the adopted child lives. Online adoption has also taken much power away from the agencies. Agencies, much to their consternation, can no longer procrastinate local adoptions for the yearly period required in order that the child be eligible for foreign adoption, nor falsify the necessary three rejection slips from Indian families required for a child to also become a candidate for inter-country adoption. Lastly, they are unable now to leave some parents on endless wait lists, usually non-Hindus, while favoring Hindu perspective clients. Lastly, hopefully it will be much more difficult for adoption agencies to accept the traditional bribes allowing some families to be favored over others.

This notwithstanding, online adoption also has its drawbacks. Most of the children who are being considered for adoption come from rural areas. All the online adoption applications are only in English, so it is with great apprehension that many of the less educated and less sophisticated become involved in the system. Thus, today adoption is becoming more and more an urban phenomena and the prospective parents are often from the middle socio-economic class and sometimes even from an upper one.

Otherwise, in order to adopt a child, the consent of both parents is required and when a couple is adopting, they have to be married for at least two years, a single female can also adopt a child of either gender, while a single male can only adopt a male child. However, LGBTs, that is lesbians, gays, bisexual and transgenders cannot adopt an Indian child at all. When the child is up to four-years-old, the maximum composite age of the parents is ninety and the maximum age of a single prospective parent is forty-five. When the child is above four up to eight, the maximum composite age of the parents is hundred years and the maximum age of a single prospective parent is fifty, and finally, when the child is above eight up to eighteen, the maximum composite age is one hundred and ten years and the maximum age of a single prospective parent is fifty-five. The minimum age between the child and either of the prospective parents should not be less than twenty-five years and couples with more than four children are not eligible to adopt.

Yet, apart from these very basic guidelines is the fact that Indians are not used to stranger adoption and when they make the 'leap' too often they only want 'the perfect child' or no child. For every child who gets adopted there are ten others who are deemed 'non-adoptable'. Although they may be technically eligible for adoption they do not fit into the 'dream child' category, that is either they have health problems whether mental, emotional or physical, they have dark skin, they are older children that is beyond the age of four and sometimes even two or are part of a sibling set. The children, however, often find homes abroad where families have learned to be more flexible. One also must remember that it was only hundred years ago that the state accepted to take the responsibility for destitute and abandoned children by the Children's Act which was enacted in the Madras and Bombay Presidencies in 1920. While Chinese orphans have always been stigmatized, in India, once again, it seems their image is even worse because they are furthermore regarded as 'bad' children in need of punishment which is certainly no aid in encouraging prospective parents who need motivation to adopt them.

Simultaneously, those Indians who finally do adopt are advised by the agencies to tell the adoptee about their adoption. In many cases, however, parents are very hesitant to inform their children. Some never learn of their adoption because once again stranger adoption is just beginning to be accepted at all, and even close family members are unaware of the situation. Otherwise, parents are also fearful that should a child learn that the adopted parents are not the birthparents, this could alienate the child from them as well as destabilize the adoptee. In other cases, adoptive parents plan to apprise the adoptee at some point, but find it difficult to have the courage to tell him.

Otherwise, adopted children in general go through stages regarding their adoption. These phases are probably more intense when the child, for example, an Indian does not physically resemble the birthmother, and she is constantly aware of her difference. Most children think and fantasize about the birthmother as early as three or four years old, they invent games involving a missing or stolen mother. It is usually also during the pre-school years that the families tell their children that they are adopted. Often, after a couple of years, around five to seven they are however more overtly inquisitive about the birthmother and begin to have a real awareness of the meaning of adoption. This may create a sense of confusion and insecurity because many children come to question their permanence in the family. However, around eight the child really begins to feel the loss related to her adoption because she becomes cognizant that the birthmother could not look after her and abandoned her. She realizes that the birthmother lives in India and wants to understand more about her relinquishment. As synthesized by D.M. Brodzinsky: "Now this child can infer the flip side of her beloved 'adoption story'—that for her to have been chosen, she first had to have been given away".[7] At this age and during the pre-adolescent years, the child is hurt, pained and angry. She usually becomes sulky and withdrawn and is often subject to temper tantrums. The negative feelings she feels toward her birthmother, she furthermore projects onto her mother. Studies have furthermore demonstrated that 'deep psychic pain' and 'narcissistic wounds' also emerge for the adoptive mother when the adoptee speaks to her about the birthmother. Additionally, many of these adoptees also have a fear of rejection and a fear that their basic needs will not be accounted for. In any case, the child is then driven by anger as well depicted by Betty Jean Lifton:

> Anger, the other side of depression, is always waiting to be tapped in the adoptee.... Anger that adoptees have built up over the years can erupt as uncontrollable rage. There is the unexpressed anger that they are adopted;

7. D.M. Brodzinsky and M.D. Schechter eds., *Being Adopted: The Lifelong Search for Self* (New York: Doubleday, 1992), 18.

> anger that they are different; anger that they are powerless to know their origins; anger that they cannot express their real feelings in a family climate of denial. When this anger is allowed to build in a child over the years, it will eventually surface as aggression—stealing, setting fire, destroying property—and if left unresolved, as violence.[8]

At this particular stage, it is advised that the adopted mother remains as close as possible to her daughter empathizing with her and openly discussing the birthmother and even helping the child to identify with her and to imagine her. It seems the more the birthmother becomes a reality, the less subconsciously she haunts the daughter. While these years are considered among the most problematic, puberty and adolescence come with another set of problems. The pubescent adoptee often awakens in the adoptive parents' feelings of failure connected with their infertility. Many times, this arouses sentiments of envy and even jealousy relating to the adopted child's budding sexuality and fertility. This in turn is a factor which frequently creates stress between parent and child. Meanwhile, during adolescence, the problems encountered are mainly related to the adoptee's sense of identity. Not only are the adoptees concerned with their personal identity, but also their racial and cultural ones; in a word these girls need to know who they are. In any case, especially these interracial and inter-country adoptees are faced with 'genealogical bewilderment', that is a state of confusion and uncertainty in a child who has either no knowledge or only uncertain knowledge of her natural parents. 'Genealogical bewilderment' can additionally lead to low self-esteem and an unclear sense of identity. Thus, beginning in adolescence, these children, particularly those who are not completely satisfied in their adoptive homes, begin to consider seriously the possibility of finding out and even searching for their birth families. Yet, active searching does not usually begin until the late twenties or early thirties and sometimes not until the adoptees have children, themselves. Searchers are in the minority and even though in

8. Sherrie Eldidge, *Twenty Things Adopted Kids Wish Their Adoptive Parents Knew* (N.Y.: Random House, 1999), 66.

the past this was considered unacceptable, more recently most professionals and lawyers assist in contacting the birth families when they are in agreement.

As in China and elsewhere, some adopted children from India need also to discover their roots. They hope to obtain answers to some of the eternal questions such as how and when did they end up in an orphanage? Who were their parents? Were they orphaned? Were they abandoned? Were they trafficked? Arun Dohle was adopted from a Pune orphanage by a German couple when he was an infant. It took him a court order and seventeen seemingly endless years of searching until he finally located his mother and learned that he was given up for adoption without his mother's consent; the adoption arranged by an influent politician. Arun now assists other adoptees to find their biological families which is for them both financially and emotionally a large commitment. In the case of trafficked children, the search becomes next to impossible because the records have been falsified.

Interestingly, for Indian adoptees living in India, it is almost non-existent for them to search for their birthparents. This is explained by the fact that Indians move very rarely and tend to place roots where they live, making the child feel more secure with his family and environment. Another hypothesis is that it is also possible that the adoptee believes that the birth family came from a lower caste, so he does not want to investigate his past. Those adoptees living abroad, by contrast, often tend to have experienced a more open attitude toward adoption, giving them the incentives to search. This notwithstanding, it has been noted that most adoptive parents feel uncomfortable when their adopted child evokes the need to search for his biological family. The adopted family, although they do not always express it, becomes riddled with sentiments of fear, anger, and insecurity. On the one hand, they feel rejected and on the other, they worry that they could lose the adoptee.

Two movies have also been made on the subject of searching for one's biological family, *Manufactured Orphans* and the 2016 award-winning film, *Lion*. *Manufactured Orphans* was based on the search of Jyoti Svahn, a twenty-three-year-old living in

Sweden who was adopted from a well-recognized orphanage in Bangalore. With the aid of Arun, she found out that her mother had left her and her sister temporarily for orphanage care but had died. Meanwhile, her father already separated from her mother was still living. *Lion* was based on the life story of Saroo Brierley, another Indian adoptee who returned to India from Australia in search of his biological family. Saroo found out that he was the son of a single mother who was a construction worker in West Bengal. When he was five, he had fallen asleep on an empty compartment of a train and got lost. He was found on a street and admitted to a children's home. He finally re-united with his mother in 2013 after arduous searching.

As adoptive parents were already plagued by adoption issues mainly psychological, social or legal ones, support groups were originally founded in Mumbai and Pune. Later, in 1995, the Alternative Parent Network Association (APNA) was launched in New Delhi. The activities of the group include social events, parental meetings as well as workshops for both children and parents in Delhi. These groups have opened in other cities such as Chennai and Bangalore in order to assist families to overcome the frequent isolation involved in adoption.

With so many practical and emotional difficulties still involved in adoption, in October 2014, two women, Srobona Das and Swarna Venkataraman started a private Facebook group entitled For & Of Heart Babies (FOHB) in order to launch an online support group and community of adoptive parents in India. The group is constantly growing and counts today one thousand and seventy-two members from many Indian cities, including those who are on the verge of adopting, some even living abroad. They help each with a plethora of problems from very basic ones like filling in the cumbersome application forms to handling some of the very delicate questions sometimes asked by an adoptee. They also discuss issues such as how to convince spouses to adopt, given that they are often unfamiliar and uncomfortable with stranger adoption. Probably, too, this support group ultimately acts as a form of reinforcement for those parents who have already made the leap to adopt.

Foster care, a system practiced throughout the world, is another means by which the adoption scheme is being rejuvenated. The Service Center in Mumbai was the first to place Indian children in foster care in 1971. Foster care, a pet scheme of WCO Minister Maneka Gandhi was legalized in India through the Juvenile Justice (Care and Protection) Act 2014. Until recently, only children in orphanages have been placed for adoption, by this system abandoned and surrendered children, while they await an adoption home, can be allocated to foster families. The families are usually middle income. The government provides the foster family with a maximum sum of 2,500 rupees a month. However, one of the criteria on which they are selected is that they are financially comfortable and do not need to rely on the money allotted to them. There is also a provision for group foster care in which a family can provide for more than one child, but no more than two. The families are generally from the middle and sometimes even lower income bracket. They are responsible for the children's education, health, food and general well-being. Foster care ends when the child is eighteen but can be extended to twenty-one. Meanwhile, the time frame of fostering is almost always unknown; it can be short, medium or long term. The foster family has additionally the first right of adoption after a five-year period and it is only if the child is adopted that he has the same legal rights as a biological child. For children it is preferable to institutional care which has thus far proven to be deleterious both emotionally and mentally to the child. Among the children who can benefit from the program are those under seven years of age who have not been adopted after a minimum of one year of being declared legally free for adoption, children whose parents are mentally ill and unable to care for the child, children having one or both parents in jail, children whose parents submit a request to the government asking to surrender their child due to terminal illness or children whose families are temporarily unable to provide for them. Meanwhile, the foster care parents must be Indian citizens, both above the age of thirty-five having an income whereby they can provide for the child. They need to be in good health and show proof of not having HIV, TB or Hepatitis B.

Lastly, they must be without criminal conviction or indictment. Since Independence, with increased urbanization, many Indian families have moved from joint families to nuclear ones. Foster care is in a way replacing the role played by extended families. Foster Care India has been the most active organization in promoting this form of child care. It is based in Rajasthan and has placed children with success in that area. It has also created consciousness and has influenced policy making. As of now, however, there are some organizations that place children in foster care; Kerala has fourteen and Maharashtra has eight. Yet, previously, the only stipulation which one can seriously question is why the program limits itself to children under seven years old when there are so many older children in the same predicament.

The SOS Children's Villages in India began in 1964. Kinderoff International is a private Austrian charity which already thirty years ago operated all over the world with more than three hundred SOS Villages in a hundred countries. Similar to the ones in China and other parts of the world, in India they are also another form of foster care. Presently, there are thirty-two SOS Children's Villages in twenty-two states in India. There are six thousand five hundred children living in SOS Villages. Each village has twelve to fifteen family homes, with each home consisting on an average of ten children, where they live without the possibility of adoption with an SOS mother, brothers and sisters until they grow up. SOS Villages in India always remain a charity and provide for children who are considered the most vulnerable, those who are the children of widows, single women and from families below the poverty line. The program operates day-care centers, kindergartens, schools and vocational training centers as well as medical centers.

According to the Juvenile Justice Act, children who are considered to be distressed fall in one of two categories: those in conflict with the law and those who need care and protection. The act mandates child care institutions in every district. Yet, many of these homes under the auspices of the federal and state governments and the NGOs are emblematic of abuse, especially of a sexual nature. Children, both male and female, are frequently raped, usually by staff or older boys. They have furthermore been made to live in completely inhuman situations and many are even sold. For example, at Apna Ghar, a child care institution in Rohtak, more than a hundred female residents claimed that they were raped by caretakers and outsiders for more than a year. Children were furthermore filmed for pornography and more than a dozen were sold. A great number of these institutions where sexual abuse has been reported are registered under laws, such as the Societies Registration Act, the Charitable and Religious Trusts Act, the Women and Children Institutions Act, but not under the Juvenile Justice (JJ) Act. In fact, many of the homes and orphanages are not registered at all, and thus they avoid government and police inspection. However, Maneka Gandhi appealed to state adoption bodies to ensure that all orphanages were registered under the Juvenile Justice Act, 2015, before the end of 2017. She reported that four thousand of the total nine thousand child care institutions were still not registered under the JJ Act and were thus operating illegally. She also stated that forty thousand boys and girls were abiding in these unregistered homes. Gandhi's constant attention to these issues will certainly pay off.

The orphanage Preet Mandir, which is based in Pune, created one of the largest scandals in India. Its owner, Jogindev Singh Bhasin; his wife, his son and other colleagues including even the former chairman of the New Delhi-based CARA, J.K. Mittal, were charged for their involvement in a major adoption racket. Although they were granted bail in 2011, in 2013 Preet Mandir's license was not re-newed as a result of the corrupt activities since 2002. The main culprits were Bhasin and his immediate family who were accused for misappropriating funds for their personal use to the level of 47 lakh (47,000,00 rupees) for travelling expenses, sojourns in five-star hotels and luxury goods including a ruby and diamond necklace with matching earrings, which Bhasin generously gave to his wife mainly from illegal donations made to the orphanage. Otherwise, the family was charged under various sections of the Penal Code for criminal conspiracy, cheating, forgery, kidnapping, extortion, misappropriation of property, criminal breach of trust, and falsification of accounts. The orphanage almost systematically falsified the necessary three rejection slips for Indian families in order to send the children abroad which is always a much more lucrative adoption. Worse yet, when poor families in particular brought their children to the orphanage to lodge and educate them for a period of time, as is the custom in India, Bhasin would have them sign papers whereby unknowingly they were instead giving them up for adoption, which is in fact a form of kidnapping. When the parents returned to recuperate them, they were often residing in another part of the world.

However, Bhasin's activities were not only involved with Preet Mandir, he had a second organization, a rehabilitation center, one equivalent to a crisis pregnancy center in the United States. Sai Dham at Kanhe Phata in Mulshi Taluka was alleged to rehabilitate unwed mothers and distressed women having family problems. It was also supposed to educate illiterate and poor women. While no counseling of any kind was given to the women, sixty-nine surrender agreements were obtained from unwed mothers whose children were brought to Preet Mandir for adoption; the center ultimately a means to procure children.

Finally, in 2010, CARA had suspended Preet Mandir's license for irregularities in sending children for inter-country adoption. At that time, there were already eighteen adoptions from Preet Mandir in the pipeline. CARA recommended that the applications be processed in the best interests of the children. The Supreme Court granted CARA their requests. Given Preet Mandir's history, it seems that there should have been a case by case investigation because many of these children could have been kidnapped with distressed parents in search of them. Secondly, with the then five thousand and now ten thousand Indians waiting to adopt, most of these children could have been spared international adoption and have found good homes within their own country. Furthermore, those who have children who were never surrendered for adoption and are now re-situated in adoptive families seem to have absolutely no recourse to re-cuperate them. One questions whether India should not pass a law similar to the Alba-Keneth law of 2010 in Guatemala. It required the government to create a DNA database of missing children, giving the relatives of these children the right to have their DNA analyzed.

Another adoption scandal which made headlines involved the orphanage of Malaysian Social Services (MSS) in Chennai and it furthermore became part of Scott Carney's book, *On the Trail of the World's Organ Brokers, Bone Thieves, Blood Farmers and Child Traffickers.* In fact, the orphanage was implicated in more than one hundred cases of kidnapping for profit. From 1991 through 2003, according to the documents filed by the Chennai police, it also arranged one hundred and sixty-five international adoptions, mostly to the United States, the Netherlands and Australia, earning some $ 250,000 in orphanage fees; of these, many of the kidnapped children were a part.

One of the most heartbreaking stories involved the kidnapping of Subash, the toddler son of Sivagama and Nageshwar Rao, a construction painter in Chennai, by the orphanage's gardener. Subash was kidnapped off the Chennai slums when his mother left him for only a moment by the neighborhood water pump. He was adopted two years later by an American family in the Midwest. Subash was particularly adoptable with his light skin and good health.

The poor slum family spent their life savings to find their son, even taking their daughter out of school. Furthermore, Sivagama was subject to a long-term depression. After many years of searching, Subash was miraculously tracked down. Afterwards, Carney, himself, went to the Midwest to speak to the adopted family and try to establish some form of dialogue between the two families at one level or another, but the American family was very resistant and refused even a DNA sample. On the one hand, they were in denial but on the other hand they were fearful that Subash could be taken away from them. This is a classic case when children are trafficked and the biological parents who are usually much poorer also have no recourse.

The orphanage is owned by the Ravindranath family. After Ravindranath's death in 2006, it was taken over by his son,

Dinesh. When interviewed by Scott Carney, he completely distorted the truth stating that the scandals were blown out of proportion and he claimed to be the victim of the police who were trying to extort funds from the orphanage. When Carney tried to have him explain the fees given to the kidnappers, he justified the expenditure by stating that sums of two to three thousand rupees were paid to those who brought children to the orphanage as a gesture of good will; however, they were in fact kidnappers and were being paid much more, somewhere near $ 236.

Dinesh and many of the other orphanage owners should pay a much steeper price such as life imprisonment or the death sentence, possibly this could make them and all the other traffickers afraid to further venture into this activity. Instead, although MSS closed the orphanage and is no longer involved in international adoptions, ironically it still runs a few social programs and a school for young children, all of which is approved by the Indian Government.

Another well-known scandal was the Lambada scandal which broke out in March and April 1999. It involved Sanjeeva Rao and his orphanage, Action for Social Development (ASD); Rao having already been involved in other orphanage irregularities. Peter Subbaiah, the orphanage head of the Good Samaritan Evangelical and Social Welfare Association was also implicated and for once they were both arrested and imprisoned. They bought baby girls through intermediaries from the Lambada tribe in Andhra Pradesh. While these scouts or intermediaries bought the girls for $ 15 to $ 45, they resold them for larger sums such as $ 220 to $ 240 to the orphanages. When a woman became pregnant, they struck a deal whereby if the child was a girl, she would be bought while if a boy he would remain with his family. Lambada children were particularly saleable since they have fair complexions and are thus particularly appealing for India's in-country adoption market. The Lambada were historically a nomadic tribe who have now settled into hamlets called *tandas*. They maintained themselves through farming and manual labor, yet they have remained very poor. Although the tribe initially practiced the custom of a bride price, they now have adopted the habitual, although illegal, practice of dowry. The Lambada were also renown for believing that if the third, sixth or ninth child was a girl that she was inauspicious. Consequently, they were prone to infanticide or if not also selling the baby girls for a very modest price. Meanwhile, the orphanages resold them for $ 2,000 to $ 3,000. When Rao and Subbaiah were temporarily imprisoned, efforts were made to reunite these children with their original families, but these attempts were generally fruitless, their families not wanting them back.

David Smolin, Professor of Law at Cumberland Law School at Stanford University and the adoptive father of two Indian girls involved in another adoption scandal, rightly recommended that a financial cap be placed and enforced on these international adoptions in order to curb the large appetites of traffickers who are selling their human produce on the international adoption market. Otherwise, and importantly he opines that the receiving countries are in state of denial and not taking any responsibility for the children coming from the sending countries and he believes this too needs to be corrected:

> No American company providing customer services to Americans through a call center in India could disclaim responsibility for private violations, sloppy work, or rudeness, because "we can't control what happens in India." No American company employing software programmers or financial analysis in India could avoid fundamental ethical norms because "we can't stop corruption in India". No importer of goods into the United States would be permitted to disclaim product liability responsibility for defective products based on the argument that "we can't control the way things are made in China". In a connected, interdependent world, it is normative that professionals, organizations, and industries involved in cross-border work are responsible for the integrity and quality of the service or good, regardless of how many nations were networked and involved in providing or creating the service or good. Responsibility for adoption is not less significant or

> important than these other responsibilities, and there is no reason that institutions and individuals working in adoption services should be able to disclaim their normal responsibilities in such a brazen fashion.[9]

Even though India has been riddled with adoption scandals and corruption, in some cases, fortunately, the opposite is also true; such an example is Prakash Kaur Bibi's Unique Home for Girls in Jalandhar, Punjab. She started the children's home when she was twenty-four in 1993. Bibi was, herself, abandoned as a child by her biological parents and grew up in another home for girls, also in Jalandhar. Her shelter lodged sixty girls within five rooms and a small courtyard. Since the beginning, she has been rescuing abandoned baby girls and even has a cradle outside her house. Most of the babies when found are somewhere between a life and death situation and are rushed immediately to the hospital. When the infants return to her home, Bibi and the older girls diligently nurse them back to health. Although initially it was next to impossible to even feed all the incoming children, already in 1993 local well-wishers formed the Bhai Ghanayya Ji Charitable Trust to assist in maintaining the home. The main trustee is Bibi, herself. The other trustees include doctors and businessmen from the Jalandhar community. Over time, the Unique Home has become renown and is furthermore subsidized by wealthy Punjabi and other Indians throughout the country and even some individuals from other parts of the world. Consequently, in 2016, Bibi and her adopted family moved to a three-storey bungalow with light-filled rooms and landscaped gardens. The new facilities have separate suites for Bibi's married 'daughters' who frequently visit their adopted mother.

In the home everyone wakes up at 5:30 AM, the older girls assisting the younger ones to get ready for school; the schools always among the best. At noon the girls return for lunch and in the evening, tutors come to help with extra courses and their

9. David Smolin, "The Two Faces of Intercountry Adoption: The Significance of the Indian Adoption Scandals", *Seton Hall Law Review,* 35, No. 2 (2005), 492.

homework. Weekends, however, are reserved for play as well as occasional visits not only to fast-food restaurants but even good ones. The girls furthermore have a collective birthday in April with a hundred-kilogram cake, a sign that the home is heavily endowed. During the summer, they are furthermore taken to the hills outside the city. Otherwise, much focus is placed upon their education. One of the daughters, for instance, is studying medicine in the UK, while another has her master's degree in education. For those who prefer not to pursue higher education or a career and wish instead to get married and have a family, 'Mama' Bibi manages to find them a suitable partner. On her website Bibi appropriately discourages parents from abandoning their girls: "Don't abandon your daughters; not everyone is lucky enough to reach the Unique Home", and unique it is.

As summarized by Vinita Bhargava, Head of the Department of Child Development at University of Delhi, "Adoption is a second choice, exercised when God lets you down."[10] Although adoption existed in India as far back as Hindu mythology, for centuries as in China it has existed within the context of the immediate or extended family. With increasing urbanization, adoption is now becoming stranger adoption. Most Indians often strongly embedded in Hinduism and the caste system are frequently fearful to take this step into the unknown which is one of the reasons for India's extremely low adoption rates. Child laundering is another major reason why people have become apprehensive in front of adopting from India since the country has become the hub of rampant trafficking. To diminish this problem, it is crucial that the foreign adoption fees are proportionate to the local economics. As well synthesized by Thomas DiFilipo, president of the Joint Council on International Children's Services, "Unless you control the money, you won't control the corruption."[11]

---

10. Vinita Bhargava, *Adoption in India: Policies and Experiences* (New Delhi: Sage Publications India Pvt Ltd., 2005), 50.
11. E.J. Graff, "The Lie We Love", 66.

Chapter 3

China's Male-dominated Society: A Historical View

Chinese society was originally matriarchal, but by the time of Xia dynasty China first became patriarchal and has remained so until, ironically, the time of Mao Zedong's dictatorship. His 1950 Marriage Law, propagated female equality at home and the workplace. This law, as well as many others he passed in defense of women's rights, allowed them to see a light at the end of the tunnel. However, with the government's later fear of an uncontrollable population explosion, the One-child policy came into effect in 1980. The flagrant increase in sex-selection abortion and female infanticide and abandonment was an uncontestable manifestation of the country's ingrained belief in male superiority. Yet, China is now paying the price of its misogyny and is left with a current generation of male singletons who are *guanggun* or 'bare branches', biological dead ends, searching for a mate who will produce an heir.

The Chinese who lived along the Yellow River seven thousand years ago were ironically part of a matrilineal society of hunter-gatherers. Not only was descent transmitted through the woman's family, but men also inhabited their wives' homes and all the children were given their mother's name.

However, by the Xia dynasty (c. 2100–c. 1600 BC), Chinese society had stabilized, the men were no longer itinerant and had instead become farmers. China then became a patrilineal society whereby descent was traced through the male line and women once married lived in their husbands' home. It was then, too, the Chinese began ancestor worship, which could only be performed by the male descendants. Importantly, the Xia dynasty marked the beginning of male supremacy.

By the Feudal Age (1100-221 BC), male superiority and female subordination had become fully ingrained in Chinese society. The *Book of Changes*, the *I Ching,* relegated a woman unconditionally to her home and family, while a man worked and functioned freely in the outside world. It was during this period that women could no longer inherit family property, which instead could only be bequeathed to the wife's elder brother or to her eldest son. When there were no sons, the property was inherited by a male who was part of the extended family. During the sixth and fifth century BC, the politician and philosopher, Confucius furthermore established a family system based on male lineage. He advocated that all the land, money, and other family possessions be transmitted from father to son. Confucius also strongly devalued women, equating them quite simply with people of low birth. Later, during the fifth and fourth centuries BC, Mencius reinforced his mentor's position. According to him, not producing a male heir was the greatest manifestation of unfilial behavior. This attitude, particularly in rural China, is strongly prevalent even today.

China's misogynous beliefs continued to be upheld throughout the centuries and reached an apex during the Song dynasty (960-1279 AD) with the custom of child brides and foot binding. A child bride was placed in a particularly vulnerable position. Girls who were the offspring of poor families were sold into wealthier ones who had sons. The girls were usually twelve or thirteen, while the future husbands were surprisingly much younger, usually three or four and sometimes still babies of six months. Meanwhile, these girls were much reviled by their in-laws and treated like slaves within the family. When the boys grew up, they married the girls and their family conveniently avoided the habitual weddings with their huge expense. Beginning in the eleventh century and lasting as late as 1901, the cruel practice of foot-binding was also established in order that women were crippled and imprisoned within their homes. Only peasant girls escaped this brutal tradition because they had to work in the home and the fields. The others as of five or six-years-old were systematically the victims of this ruthless custom; those who did not bind their feet were unable to find an appropriate mate.

During the Ming (1368-1644) and Qing (1644-1911) dynasties, an obsessive premium was further placed on a woman's chastity. Consequently, wives and even concubines were supposed to kill themselves before their husbands or lovers went to war, in order to avoid their potential infidelity. Otherwise, wives and concubines were to kill themselves or be killed after a husband's or lover's death. When a woman's fiancé died, she was reduced to marrying a wooden tablet and to remain single for the rest of her life. She was also assigned to the role of servant in her fiancé's family, even if she had never met him. Today, these feudal attitudes still linger, and some men will not marry unless a doctor guarantees their future wife's virginity.

Women's increasing enslavement continued until Mao, believing that "women hold up the sky", treated them as equal to men. After the establishment of the People's Republic, very significantly, he passed the Marriage Law of 1950, which gave women the possibility to choose their husbands, to ask for a divorce, to inherit property, to use their own family names, and to have an equal position in both the workplace and the home. Women from the All-China Women's Federation as well as the justice department were sent throughout China, explaining this new law to the people. He also outlawed prostitution, child marriage, the taking of concubines, the selling of brides, female infanticide and abandonment. Mao furthermore fought the flagrant issue of female illiteracy whereby even peasant girls were given the possibility of education.

However, by 1980, with the enactment of the One-child policy and the consequent increase in female infanticide and abandonment of baby girls as well as the augmentation of women's abuse in general, Mao's propagation of female equality was strongly undermined. The Family Planning Policy was enacted following China's greatest famine, its purpose was to limit the country's population expansion and the birth plan was forecasted to terminate after one generation. However, it was only in 2016 that the birth policy was even amended, then allowing all Chinese to have only two children instead of one.

The policy was particularly rigid in urban areas. Yet, beginning even as early as 1980, official policy made exceptions for 'practical difficulties' such as both children being only children or for parents whose offspring had a physical or intellectual disability, a mental illness, or who died. During the 1980s, this birth plan was also eased in rural areas; families who already had a girl were allowed another child which alone demonstrates the population's persistent 'son preference'. Otherwise, other exceptions were made, among them for non-Han ethnic groups and Han Chinese living in the countryside. By 2007 as much as 53% of the population virtually all rural, were allowed two children, while another 36%, almost all urban, were still the victims of China's very rigorous birth plan. Nevertheless, in a 2008 survey, amazingly, it was recorded that 76% of the Chinese people supported the birth policy. However, it was still very controversial outside the country.

However, as there are no penalties for multiple births, many couples, especially affluent ones, have been trying to avoid the One-child policy by giving birth to twins or even triplets. According to a 2006 *China Daily*, the yearly number of multiple births had doubled. Women were having twins by using fertility drugs, or by registering non-twin children as twins. In Shanghai, according to recent statistics, one in every fifty babies are twins. Yet, the most unparalleled example of this is the story of a successful businesswoman from Quangzhou who in 2010 produced eight children within a month. She was nicknamed *babantoi muquin*, or China's Octomom. She, too, produced her tribe of offspring through the aid of two surrogate mothers and fertility treatments, giving birth to several children herself. She is alleged to have spent not far from $ 160,000 in fertility treatments, surrogacy and medical expenses, not to speak of the fees incurred by the eleven nannies. In order to avoid being hounded by the media, she and her family went into hiding but after two years of investigation, the couple was subject to substantial fines.

Upon marriage, a couple was also required to sign an agreement stating that they would adhere to the birth quotas. Those who consented could be allowed a Birth Planning Honor Card, which allowed them special benefits for food, medical care, housing and also education. Some urban families were also given a monthly stipend upon retirement. Those who refused even under constant persuasion were subject to punishment by fines, loss of benefits or jobs and even imprisonment. Furthermore, in order to conceive and bear a child, a woman was required to have a *Shengyn zheng*, a 'birth permission'. This permit gave her the official right to conceive and bear a child and she was also required to bring it to the hospital at the time of delivery. Women, who did not abide by these laws were also in jeopardy of imposed abortions as late as the eighth or ninth month of pregnancy placing the woman's life at stake.

At the peak of the birth planning campaign, China became a form of police state that reached unlimited proportions. In some places, women's menstrual cycles were posted on the workplace. Should they become pregnant with an over-quota child, they could be dragged violently from their home in the middle of the night and injected with drugs that would kill the fetus. Otherwise, a birth would be punished with hefty fines and sterilization. Women who tried to convince birth control officials to allow them to keep their unborn or born children were scornfully alluded to as 'pleaders'. Out-of-plan children could also not be enrolled in schools nor receive state services. Meanwhile, boxes were also placed throughout the community where informants could anonymously apprise government officials of those attempting to conceal a pregnancy. Nevertheless, after the birth of a second child, couples, usually the woman, underwent forced sterilization. However, finally, by 2002, the government did finally outlaw the use of physical force to coerce a woman to undergo either an abortion or sterilization. Yet, as many of the other laws, this one, too, was little enforced. In the ultimate analysis, the only Chinese that managed to escape these draconian restrictions were the wealthy who bribed the authorities and managed to have a desired number of children; these extra children even becoming a status symbol. In major cities such as Beijing and Shanghai, parents paid the equivalent of three years' salary for an additional child; these children were sometimes even named according to the amount of the fine paid, 'Little One Thousand', as an example.

Because of the frequent sex-selected abortions, 95% of the aborted fetuses being systematically female, by 1987, doctors were forbidden to reveal to parents the sex of their child through ultrasound testing, etc. However, the rule was very little respected. Medical practitioners were easily bribed being usually paid an amount somewhere between $ 35 to $ 50; in some cases, even a pack of cigarettes sufficed. Consequently, in the beginning of 1994, China implemented a new law that, except when absolutely necessary to the mother's health, forbade doctors to administer any form of test designed to identify a child's gender; this included ultrasound scan, amniocentesis, chromosome test, etc. Medical practitioners who failed to abide by the law and were caught more than twice had their license automatically cancelled. Concurrently, even the mother was punished and was not allowed to give birth to her first child before five years and worse yet, was never allowed to have a second one. Fines were another form of punishment. While many of the wealthy urban population could afford to pay the imposed penalty if they were caught, the rural poor were unable to assume the costs. In any case, these sex-selected abortions were another manifestation of the pressure placed on a woman to bear a son, particularly when she was only allowed one, and only one.

During this period, pornography, prostitution and the slave trade of women also spread rampantly. The National People's Congress claimed that the authorities had investigated over eighteen thousand cases of the sale of women in 1990, and that in 1989 and 1990, over sixty-eight thousand were arrested for trafficking in women and children. Not only were girls bought and sold as brides by their families, but there were large criminal rackets organized by gangs that kidnapped and sold young girls to brothels. Again, from 1989 to 1990, police rescued ten thousand kidnapped girls throughout China. Apart from traffickers, themselves, normal, healthy children, in particular, were also frequently the victims of unethical doctors. Zhang

Shuha, a doctor at the Maternal and Child Health Hospital in Shanxi Province was a salient example. He informed one couple that their children had incurable diseases and advised them to abandon the children. He afterwards, sold them to traffickers, but was later sentenced to death for child trafficking. Today, with increasing modernization, awareness and the implementation of a systematic two children policy, a female's position is, however, gradually improving.

The One-child policy has furthermore created a very serious gender imbalance in China. In 2004, it reached its peak when there were 121 boys to every 100 girls. By 2020 it is predicted that there will be thirty to forty million, surplus men. Consequently, *caili*, a kind of reverse dowry, is given to the bride's family. In rural areas, over a long period of time, there has been a mutual exchange of gifts and money; the bride price paid by the groom's family and a dowry paid by the bride's family. Usually, *caili* is more substantial, a reflection of a woman's actual worth as housewife, cook, sex partner and mother. *Caili* has only recently become an urban phenomenon. Cities with the highest *caili* are Shanghai and Tianjin at $ 16,000 and $ 9,600, respectively.

Many parents of these children were the victims of the 'Cultural Revolution' which took place during 1966-76. Even their secondary education was interrupted, the government sending them either to the countryside, or to the factories to be 're-educated'. Consequently, many now live vicariously through their child, placing an enormous premium on his or her education and also pampering the child with all the amenities they lacked, themselves. Thus, parents most readily help a son, despite the soaring market, to buy an apartment in order to enhance his eligibility. This is commonly referred to as "building a nest to catch a phoenix".[1] Yet, despite their parents' unconditional support, some desperate young men for $ 5,000 and up have resorted to sex-dolls to compensate for their lack of a feminine presence. These outrageously expensive inflatable life size five-foot dolls are steel-jointed skeletons covered with

1. Mei Fong, *One Child: The Story of China's Most Radical Experiment.* (London: Clays Ltd., 2016), 117.

pliable PVC flesh which are created to appear as authentic as possible. By 2014, sex-dolls were being produced at a mass market rate of $ 3,000 and were thus more accessible to their buyers. Some forlorn, horny male singletons are using these dolls as substitute companions while despairingly awaiting the possibility of a human soul mate. Other 'Little Emperors' are relentlessly pursuing computer dating services and are active followers of matchmaking TV programs such as "We Meet Tonight".

Yet, even upon the onset of the birth planning policy, the government feared this potential sex imbalance. Later, it appointed the All-Women's Federation to convince families of the equality of the sexes. Posters and other forms of advertisements, as well as campaigns, such as the 2003 Care for Girls campaign, were launched in the hopes of promoting a female's image. By 2004, the government's fear had become a reality, when millions of girls could not be accounted for. At this time, the Communist Party also mobilized the State Family Planning Commission to improve a girl's status. Parents were additionally given extra rewards in order to induce them to keep their female children. Although ultrasound testing for sex selection was already illegal, now doctors became very seriously monitored as they transported the nearly two thousand ultrasound scanners in small vans and installed them in clinics throughout the countryside. UNICEF also supported the Chinese in their campaign to enhance the position of baby girls; however, it was difficult to combat centuries of male domination.

Uncontestably, Mao's moral and legal stance with regards to women and children has left an indelible mark on the country's mentality. Yet, this notwithstanding, the Chinese, particularly those who live in rural areas, almost 80% of the population, are still extremely patriarchal and backward. There remains a definite 'son preference' which has existed for centuries. It is the son who, despite the 1950 Marriage Law, is most often the heir and inherits the family's property and land. He also does more farm work and earns more than a girl. He is additionally responsible for the family's ancestor worship, and importantly, as there are no pensions or social security in the countryside, it is the male child who takes care of his parents financially in their old age. By contrast, in the cities, a worker who has residential status is entitled to old age pensions paid by the state; these consist of at least 70% of his wages. He also has medical benefits and, in some cases, even reductions for members of his family.

A girl, instead, leaves the family and is only an economic liability because she requires a dowry. Daughters are viewed as being 'lost' or as "belonging to other people at the time of marriage". Furthermore, "the first daughter is seen as bad luck, the second a disaster, and the third as an utter catastrophe as if the whole world has fallen apart."[2] Consequently, girls receive less nutrition, medical care and education. They are also less loved than boys. Not surprisingly, they have a higher mortality rate. In some Chinese villages, families who have daughters do not even consider them as offspring. As a peasant woman recounted in the documentary *Small Happiness*: "Daughters are not family, they are only relatives."[3] A female's alleged inferiority is so ingrained, that it is even alluded to in the Chinese nursery rhyme which is equivalent to the western Mother Goose:

> We keep a dog to guard the house,
> A pig will make a feast or two;
> We keep a cat to catch a mouse;
> But what is the use of a girl like you?[4]

In ancient China, 'son preference' was already widespread. The placenta of a girl was buried outside the walls of the family home, whereas a boy's was interred within the house. Likewise, when a boy reached a couple of months, he was taken by his father to the temple who proudly apprised the gods and his ancestors of the child's birth. The family then commemorated with a full month feast; they broke out red-tinted eggs in honor

---

2. Emily Buchanan, *From China With Love: A Long Road to Motherhood* (West Sussex, England: John Wiley & Sons, 2005), 72.
3. Kay Ann Johnson, *Wanting a Daughter, Needing a Son: Abandonment, Adoption and Orphanage Care in China* (St. Paul, Minnesota: Young & Young Book Co., 2004), 4.
4. Karen Evans, *Lost Daughters of China and the Search for a Missing Past* (N.Y.: Penguin Putnam, 2000), 93.

of the son's birth. Meanwhile, when girls reached this young age, which was often not even the case, they were never given any celebration.

There are also many customs even today which support the belief in male superiority. In the countryside, as early as the time of pregnancy, boy's clothes are hung on a family's door in hopes of a male birth. When a woman actually produces a boy at the time of his '20 day' celebration, honoring his birth, he is named and given an amulet or necklace with a silver locket which he wears until he is twelve. This is also a moment in which he is particularly indulged by his maternal grandmother. Among the gifts he receives from her is a *baijiaya*—garments she has made from the remnants of clothing given to her by a hundred different families with their blessing for the newborn. To her daughter, she brings bountiful amounts of nutritious food.

For a girl, however, there is still no formal celebration. Instead, when she reaches a month, only her hair and eyebrows are shaved in the belief that they will grow back both dark and thick. Worse yet, until the turn of the century, many Chinese girls were not so much as given a name. They were called Eldest Daughter, Second Daughter, etc., names which were totally impersonal. Later, at the time of marriage, they received a combination of their father's and husband's surnames. Even Emperor Deng Xiaoping's mother was without a proper name. Now, even though girls have names, they are usually derogatory. In a peasant family, when the first born is a girl, she is sometimes called Laidi, Zhaodi or Yindi, all meaning 'bring a little brother'.

Furthermore, the poorer the villages, the greater the gender imbalance. If a woman does not give birth to a son, she is often beaten up or abandoned. Some women are also chained like dogs to the house, so they cannot escape. When she has a good track record for producing boys, sometimes her husband even rents her out to other men who want one. If she produces a boy, the husband receives 8,000 yuan, roughly $ 800. If instead she gives birth to a girl, she is either abandoned or forced to try again. In some villages, families without sons are also subject to ridicule and discrimination. They do not even receive household plots or allocations for building a new home. When women are unable to have a son, men also divorce them, so they can remarry and produce one. Finally, female abuse at all levels is rampant. In one community brothers from extremely impoverished families with no females to barter purchase a common wife, like buying an animal, in order to continue the family line. Meanwhile, one out of four women are subject to violence in the home. Thus, it was necessary for the government to pass a law in 2014 forbidding domestic violence. Not surprisingly, rural women have the highest suicide rate worldwide. With one swig of agricultural pesticide, they end all their woes.

The country's long legacy of female infanticide (child murder) has also been more widespread than in most other countries. This is another reflection of the Chinese credence in a woman's unquestionable inferiority. Otherwise, child murder generally involves the killing of unborn babies usually by drowning, starvation, suffocation, strangulation, poisoning, stabbing and even burying alive. The most common method of killing an infant is plunging the baby's head into a large pot of water and holding her head until she dies. This practice can be in part rationalized because in China an infant is not considered fully human until the age of one or has grown a full set of teeth.

At the time of the Birth Planning Policy, obstetricians in hospitals were also under government orders to kill over-quota children. They often killed the child by injecting formaldehyde or alcohol into the baby's head, or breaking the skull with the forceps as the child emerged from the birth canal. The other means which they employed were putting gauze into the baby's mouth and strangling her, or the most frequently used method was drowning the infant in a pail of water and afterwards reporting it as stillbirth.

Although infanticide diminished after the communists came to power in 1949, however, the famine, as well as the restrictive One-child policy marked its revival. By 1992, the government had even inserted a clause within the Protection of the Rights and Interests of Women stating:

> Women's right to life and health shall be inviolable. Drowning, abandoning or cruel infanticide in any manner

> of female babies shall be prohibited; discrimination against or maltreatment of women who gave birth to female babies or women who are sterile shall be prohibited....[5]

Infanticide is a criminal act which is punishable by three to ten years imprisonment. Yet, the law has very little effect in rural China. It has even been confirmed by the United States Department of State, the English Parliament and the human rights organization, Amnesty International, yet female infanticide has still not been eradicated.

Even now, in some very primitive villages, there is coercion to kill a first daughter and if the mother refuses, the village elders are convinced that they have the right to kill even the mother, herself. When girls are born, a form of soothsayer examines them, determining whether they are good looking or whether they are lucky. Villagers also go to an astrologer. He, too, judges whether she will bring good fortune. When the baby is deemed luckless, she is killed like a snake without any emotions. Much of a mother's seeming heartlessness and indifference is related to her rationalization that by killing her baby girl, she is sparing her infant all the limitless hardships she, herself, has endured as a Chinese woman.

Female infanticide has attracted even the attention of some major writers such as Pearl Buck. In *The Good Earth*, she describes the strangulation of O-Lan's second daughter during the time of famine; the story being based upon a real occurrence. In *The Woman Warrior: Memories of a Girlhood Among Ghosts*, the author, Maxine Hong Kingston, also recollects being told stories of midwives who brought boxes of clean ashes by the birthing bed and suffocated the newborn baby girl in the ashes.

The abandonment of baby girls was furthermore outlawed as early as the enactment of the 1950 Marriage Law. Yet, desertion reached unimaginable proportions during the period of China's strict birth-planning program. Once again, due to the Chinese fixation on sons, a girl was mainly forsaken in the

5. Emily Buchanan, *From China With Love: A Long Road to Motherhood*, 264.

hopes of producing a boy. Otherwise, children were most often discarded because of poverty, a medical condition, a birth out of wedlock which was illegal, or a second marriage where a child from a first union was no longer wanted.

Initially, parents who did not abide by the law were fined from several hundred yuan up to a few thousand. However, by the 1990s the fines had increased, ranging from 2,000 to 5,000 yuan, the equivalent of a half a year's salary of an average worker or the penalty collected for an out-of-plan child. Otherwise, sterilization was another punishment that offenders were forced to endure. Parents also risked, and still risk, up to five years imprisonment. However, prosecutions were and have remained few and far between, since the courts are usually sympathetic to the family's economic difficulties.

On the other hand, Hong Kong has much less infant abandonment as a result of its stringent legislation and enforcement. There, parents can receive as long as ten years imprisonment. Also, when a child is born in a Hong Kong hospital and is diagnosed with an illness, the baby must remain there and continue treatment; some of the costs being absorbed by social welfare organizations.

Of the hundred thousand children abandoned per year, their parents are most often in their mid-20s to late-30s and they have an average level of education and income. 50% of the time, the husband makes the decision to desert the child and, in the other cases, 40% is a mutual decision and in 5% it is the choice of the wife. Most children are abandoned within the first six months after birth, one-third within the first two months, and a smaller percentage between six and twelve months. This phenomena occurs more frequently in the south than in other parts of the country. An infant, usually a girl, is deserted in publicly attainable locations, often near the birthparent's home. These babies can be found, for example, close to a food market, on the side of a road or a street, in a police station, under a bridge or park bench, even in a public toilet, or often in some other area easily accessible to either an orphanage or hospital. Some women even give birth in a hospital under a false name, abandoning the infant at the time of their dismissal. Otherwise, frequently children are discarded at dawn, when the weather is still cool and when there is a shorter wait for them to be found. Sometimes, firecrackers are also set off to help notify that the child has been left. In any case, they believe that the baby will be rescued by another rural family which is often the case. The mother knows, too, that when the child is found, she could otherwise be taken to a local civil affairs department, which provides for her. Meanwhile, infants can also be left on a family's doorsteps in the local vicinity; the future parents are usually childless or with only one son. In this instance, half of the abandoning parents watch, so they can know what happens to their offspring. Otherwise, these deserted girls usually have one or more sisters and no brothers. In rare instances, a note is attached to their clothes, indicating a birth date and even more rarely some form of message which could read as follows:

> This baby was born on 1992 at 5:30 a.m. and is now 100 days old.... She is in good health and has never suffered any illness. Due to the current political situation and heavy pressures that are difficult to explain, we, who were parents for these first days, cannot continue taking care of her. We can only hope that in this world there is kind-hearted person who will care for her. Thank you—In regret and shame, your father and mother.[6]

In other instances, before abandoning the child, some birth parents, mark her with small blue tattooed markings as a probable means of identifying her.

The desertion of a child is a particularly traumatic experience for a woman. She is often in denial and filled with anger, remorse as well as extreme sadness. She is subject to nightmares, phobias and depression. Furthermore, she is very poorly viewed, and she is the subject of much criticism and even ostracism. Consequently, desertion always occurs in secret, sometimes the woman giving birth in areas which are far from home. Children are also abandoned in bus or railway stations; this form of desertion being referred to as "travelling

6. Johnson, *Wanting A Daughter, Needing A Son: Abandonment, Adoption and Orphanage Care in China*, 75.

abandonment". Some of the infants are also believed to be born 'in guerrilla pregnancies' whereby a pregnant woman leaves her village and lives with friends or relatives in or near the city to give birth. If she conceives a boy, she returns to her village and registers him, but, if the baby is a girl, especially if she is disabled, the mother abandons her, returning to her village with the hopes of having a boy. In a similar vein, there also exists an "underground railway" which transports pregnant women to a place where they remain until once again hopefully, they give birth to the awaited "Messiah".

Chinese writer, Xinran, author of *The Good Women in China: Hidden Voices* interviewed some of the women who had abandoned their baby daughters. She describes their exchange near the banks of the Yangtze River, demonstrating their ability to rationalize their act with a certain resigned fatality and even some concern:

> Did they want to find out where the babies were? 'I would rather suffer this dark hole inside me if it means she can have a better life. I don't want to disturb my girl's life' said one. 'I am very pleased for a rich person to take my daughter, she has the right to have a good life', said another; 'Do you believe those foreigners who adopt our girls know how to feed and love them in their arms and hearts?'[7]

The deep emotional pain felt by a mother's abandonment of her child was also described by Xinran in an incident which occurred in 1990. In Zhangzhou, one cold winter morning, a bustling crowd had gathered around a baby girl found with a bundle of clothing in a public toilet. Barely alive, Xinran brought the baby to a nearby hospital. After having broadcast, the incident on her show, she received on her answering machine a message from the anguished mother:

> I am the mother of the baby girl. She was born just four days before you saved her. Thank you so much for taking my daughter to the hospital. I watched in the

7. Evans, *Lost Daughters of China and the Search for a Missing Past*, 164.

> crowd with my heart broken. I followed you and sat outside your radio station all day. Many, many times I almost shouted out to you: 'That is my baby!'[8]

The authorities are supposed to search the parents of deserted children for a two-month period. In the newspapers in the "Finding Announcements", they also publish a list of abandoned infants and their photographs, in order to give the biological parents the possibility of retrieving them, but this too, is almost always an exercise in futility. A finding announcement might read as follows:

> Rong Min Ying, female born 2002 Nov. 19. Picked up at the entrance of the old people's institute at Zheneun Town. At the time she was big-sized, fat and round faced.[9]

Despite the fact that in the last decade abandonment has decreased, it is still inordinately high. In order to address this continuing problem as of 2011, the Chinese Government built thirty-two baby hatches in sixteen provinces throughout the country. The hatches are the modern version of the foundling wheel begun by the Italians during the twelfth century. The baby hatches resemble large, usually pastel colored, doll houses, and are connected to a hospital or orphanage and, if not, are situated nearby them.

The first baby hatch opened in 2011 in Shijiazhuang, Hebei province. When the parents arrive, often only the mother, a button is pressed on the outside of a building, alerting the on-site nurses of their arrival. The child is deposited anonymously in an air-conditioned room comprised of a crib and incubator. When they leave the hatch, the door locks and an alarm sounds, apprising the staff of their departure. Before leaving, the grief and guilt-ridden parents, or mother, are encouraged to write down the infant's date of birth and any pertinent medical information.

---

8. Buchanan, *From China With Love: A Long Road to Motherhood,* 224.
9. *Ibid.*, 198.

The baby hatches, or 'baby safe islands' in Mandarin Chinese, are highly controversial: some insist that they protect the deserted child from death, while others claim that they promote child abandonment. Thus, outside the hatch, are very large signs condemning the practice and reminding those who violate the law that desertion is illegal. These signs are, in fact, placed to discourage any abandonment which is not absolutely essential, given that a parent who disposes of his infant in these "baby safe islands" is protected by a "safe haven" law and is not subject to prosecution.

While abandoned children during the One-child policy were primarily healthy girls, with the decreased population, the desertions over the last decade are of a different coloration. Although primarily girls, almost systematically, these infants are now the victims of serious medical problems and disabilities with which their parents are unable to cope either financially or even psychologically; these babies frequently suffering from a variety of medical disorders such as cerebral palsy, Down syndrome or congenital heart diseases, to name a few. Furthermore, only the expenses of the first child are covered and grave illnesses such as these, are not taken into account at all by the Chinese Government. By 2014, the baby hatches had received as many as one thousand and four hundred infants and were overloaded. Some closed down and others have tightened their entrance requirements, limiting the infants maximum age to one-year-old or reducing their entry hours from 9 a.m. to 5 a.m.

Chinese women and female children have for centuries been the victims of male supremacy. Even though Mao avidly defended women's rights, his faulty population (growth) and economic (agricultural to steel) policies created the country's Great Famine, which in turn forced the government to find a solution to decrease its starving population. Consequently, The Communist Party's establishment of the One-child policy which even violated human rights, ultimately propagated an increase in sex-selected abortions and female infanticide and abandonment; all means which reduced the seemingly superfluous presence of the 'weaker sex'. Today, however, the Chinese singleton male bemoans the missing females, comprising 20% of the population, who were his potential mates. He only hopes that he will not be forever destined to sex-dolls, dating services, and even the risks encountered by the illegal immigration of foreign women. Meanwhile, the existing singleton woman has been raised as an only son. She is often the male's intellectual equal and as late as graduate school, she still occupies half the class benches. Afterwards, she will, more often than not, become part of China's work force of which women now comprise as much as 70%, among the highest in Asia. She thus shares the male's career ambitions and usually refuses the traditional role of wife. She is, therefore, not even the woman he grew up to expect. He now pays the high price of patriarchy.

Chapter 4

Adoption of Children in China: Some Startling Facts

Adoption was already part of the mores and the laws in Babylonia, four thousand years ago. By the Code of Hammurabi, the oldest written law, if an adoptee dared to admit that he was adopted, his tongue was immediately cut off. Worse yet, should he furthermore search his biological parents he was blinded. If he transgressed in any way against his foster father, he was returned to his birth father. For the Hebrews and the Jews, adoption was also a customary practice in Biblical times as exemplified by the references made in the Bible to Moses as being adopted by the Pharaoh's daughter; this was actually the first recorded adoption of a transcultural and possibly even a transracial nature. Adoption in ancient China also frequently occurred but initially remained within the family or extended family; its purpose was to guarantee a male heir for spiritual and material ends. Later, stranger adoption was also practiced but has never had the same psychological impact as adoption within bloodlines. In any case, for countless generations in China the following has been true: "There are thirty-six virtues, but to be without heirs is an evil that negates them all."[1]

Historically, the main motivation of adoption was securing a male heir who could continue the ancestral sacrifices. When a family was without an heir through birth, it adopted a son within the same family or clan of the identical surname as it was considered that one of the same surnames came from an

1. Emily Buchanan, *From China With Love: A Long Road to Motherhood* (West Sussex, England: John Wiley & Sons, 2005), 65.

identical lineage. As late as the 19th century, China still practiced an ancient custom whereby a childless male was allowed to adopt the first born of any of his younger brothers because "to die without leaving a male posterity to care for his ashes and to decorate his grave thereby pacifying his wandering spirit in purgatory" was considered "one of the greatest calamities to be apprehended"[2] by a Chinese individual. All other adoptions were considered illegal. Amazingly, even posthumous adoptions were allowed if essential to guarantee that the dead father and his ancestors would continue to receive the necessary sacrifices. Thus, the early laws considered the adoption of a male 'serious' while the adoption of a female was 'trivial'.

However, by the 19th and early 20th centuries the prohibition of stranger adoption was largely ignored since lineage was no longer given its original significance. Instead, the adopted son's economic value often took precedence in the sense that he was financially responsible for his parents in their old age, once again because of the lack of social security in rural areas. Some families also preferred stranger adoption instead of adoption within the same family in order that the identity of the child's father remained concealed. This was viewed as a means of guaranteeing that the child's first loyalty was to his adopted family not to his biological one. Furthermore, adoption customarily involved a money transaction irrespective if the adoption was within the same extended family. The rationale for this was similar to the one found later in orphanages, that is that money or orphanage donations acted as a form of re-imbursement for the time, care and expenses incurred by the child prior to adoption.

Children who were adopted much less frequently outside the immediate family are described as "mulberry" insect children. This term derives from the credence that a particular form of wasp took the offspring of the mulberry insect and changed them into a young wasp and by doing so made them his progeny. Thus, like the mulberry insect, an adopted child is referred to as

2. Asha Bajpai, *Adoption Law and Justice to the Child* (Bangalore, India: National Law School of India University, 1996), 20.

mingling zi. Author, Kay Ann Johnson, furthermore argues that stranger adoption is also Confucian in the sense that, apart from lineage, Confucius also placed great emphasis on socialization rather than heredity as being crucial to a child's development.

Apart from adoption as a means of securing an heir or as a form of financial security in old age, there were many other reasons for adoption. Emperors adopted military heroes to reward them for their loyalty. Children who were left orphans, were adopted by their extended families. While China's historical and legal records demonstrate that official adoptions have principally involved males, customary adoptions include a majority of females. Girls were adopted as family servants or as future daughters-in-law, as *tongyangxi*. Both categories of adoptees were known to be very poorly treated by their adoptive families and accorded a much inferior status compared to a biological child. Half of them were adopted before the age of six months and customarily received less food, medical care and education than biological children. Worse yet, they were frequently beaten and reviled while they were being instructed to "serve" the family. Not surprisingly, many of these girls who were adopted as *tongyangxi* felt absolutely no sexual attraction toward their brothers, no less any desire to marry them. Even though today this form of marriage is forbidden, as recently as 1989, four teenage girls who were the products of these arranged marriages were reported to have drowned themselves in order to avoid their upcoming betrothal. This practice was customary in southeast China, especially on the south China coast, while not at all common in northern China. In fact, many of the adopted girls come from the south as in that part of China there exists a long tradition of adoption. In any case, the *tongyangxi* was of great convenience to the adoptive family, because the family raised her in a manner adapted to its needs, while simultaneously instilling in her undivided loyalty at a very young age. Significantly, too, the adoptive family avoided the frequently heavy wedding expenses and dowry otherwise incurred. The adoptive parents furthermore believed that her adoption could hopefully 'lead in' a son, that is enhance their possibilities of producing a son.

Meanwhile, traditionally, orphans were not the government's responsibility but a duty of the immediate family or clan. In fact, it was not until the late 19th century that Christian missionaries established orphanages in China. Additionally, if for any reason a foundling was not cared for by his extended family, another family took responsibility for him and was given a tax exemption as compensation. Furthermore, fostering was highly valued on a moral level and those who took care of these children were considered destined for salvation. In any case, an orphan's care was perceived as a duty of the community; including his food, clothing and housing and any other basic needs. In some cases, orphans were also raised in Buddhist or Taoist monasteries and, if they were ill, they were sent to foundling hospitals or government subsidized asylums with other people who also found themselves in a state of dependency such as the aged, the handicapped, the blind or the poor; all stigmatized by the irrevocability of their condition. These institutions were a form of last resort if their families were either unable or unwilling to look after them.

While abandoned children are perceived as outcasts, the orphan with both his parents deceased is in a similar position. In China, children who live in orphanages and foster care do not always have access to nutritious food, and are often also deprived of education as well as medical and dental care. Furthermore, when these children age out of the system, they are branded for life as orphans, even on their ID cards. When in China one is not issue of a respectable family, one lacks all resources to advance. A young person is even unable to register for the Gao Kao, China's version of America's SAT; since eligibility for this high school exit exam is dependent on the location of the parent's permanent residency. This examination is furthermore necessary for entrance into university, thus the child is automatically disqualified as a potential student. Additionally, he is stigmatized both professionally and personally. More often than not employers refuse to hire him, and parents do not want him to marry their children. America, as an example, is much more favorable to similar parentless and homeless children. The U.S. assist foster care youth who have aged out of the system; they by contrast are allowed the advantages of a welfare system and vocational training which give them at least a chance to overcome in part their marginality.

In ancient China children were perceived as being granted by the will of heaven and virtue was compensated by offspring, especially a male heir. By contrast, infertility was viewed as a sign of heaven's displeasure. The stigma attached to infertility still exists today and certainly influences a portion of childless couples to adopt or not: childlessness being perceived as a mortal flaw. Some Chinese adoptive parents also even conceal the adoption because they are humiliated by their infertility. Additionally, in China there is no tradition of adopting from a children's welfare center. Unlike Americans, for example, adoptive parents keep no contact with the orphanage. Some families even move three or four times after adopting in trepidation that either their adopted child or themselves will be banished from the community. With regards to the child, himself, some parents also choose to keep the adoption a secret as a means of re-enforcing the similitude between the adopted and the biological children. Certain also fear that it would make the adoptee feel insecure. When the child is abandoned, some parents believe that should he learn the truth, he would also lose his self-esteem. Other families maintain that should the child become aware of his adoption, that it would also lessen his attachment to them. Nonetheless, some parents are open with their children, but many Chinese procrastinate in discussing the issue or simply intend to never inform their adoptees at all. It is evident that in China adoption is a much more complicated and delicate issue where parents feel markedly more self-conscious and even embarrassed and exposed than in most Western nations. In any case, one can certainly deduce that in the West, particularly in America, people are more accustomed and at ease with the notion of adoption. In China, the practice until recently has been principally an informal tradition occurring mainly within the family. It is also pertinent that with the exception of the baby hatches, parents are still not able to formally give up a child to an orphanage for adoption; this inevitably also accounts for the high rate of abandonment. Although most Chinese also claim to have the same sentiments for an adoptee as a biological child, for Westerners this remains questionable. This is well expressed, in fact, by a Chinese-born head of one of the largest adoption agencies in the United States. In 1999, he declared to the *South China Morning Post*: "The concept [of adoption] hardly exists in Chinese culture. Nobody knows about it." He continues that by contrast "adoption has a long tradition in the U.S. To a Chinese if a child is not of his flesh and blood, he may not love the child as much as he loves his own child.... Americans don't feel that way." In China, it is much more difficult for an abandoned child to find a family and nurturing home because of the stigma attached to him. This journalist continues stating that "Every city in the mainland...has a social welfare home which shelters abandoned children. But few mainlanders consider adoption."[3] This is additionally clarified by a U.S. official in charge of adoption who explains in an article in the *Christian Science Monitor* that: "Would-be Chinese parents are beginning to adopt more and more, but almost all the adoptions are blood relatives.... Traditionally, Chinese have almost never adopted complete strangers."[4]

In 1995 and 1996 at the time that China was slowly opening its door to the West and particularly to the adoption of its baby girls by Westerns, Chinese orphanages became highly criticized due in part to the documentary, *The Dying Rooms: Asia's Darkest Secret,* first broadcasted in Britain in 1995 and in the U.S. in 1996, followed by the Human Rights/Asia HRW/A report in 1996. *The Dying Rooms* was a thirty-eight-minute film describing the neglect in a typical orphanage in Guangdong Province. With hidden cameras, a team of journalists covertly shot the scene of a dying orphan, appropriately called Mei Ming

3. Kay Ann Johnson, *Wanting a Daughter, Needing a Son: Abandonment, Adoption and Orphanage Care in China* (St. Paul, Minnesota: Young & Young Book Co., 2004), 137-38.
4. *Ibid.*, 138.

(no name), alone in a darkened room in a Guangdong children's welfare center. Their intention was to expose the common use of 'dying rooms' to reduce the foundling population within the country's orphanages. A number of discarded infants were also thrown together on a worn-out cot with the comment that "to be fair, they are not killing the baby girls. Rather they are not helping them to live."[5] A London newspaper, in fact, had already described a similar scenario commenting on a 'dying room' in another orphanage, this time in Nanning Guangxi Province. *The Dying Rooms* was also considered quite sensationalistic with Kate Blewett, its co-director, unwrapping a swaddled newborn in order to show her genitals as proof that it was infant girls who were victims of China's children's welfare centers after being "dump[ed] on the streets like kittens in a bag."[6] The documentary was also set in a background of eerie Oriental sounding music with even other very disturbing imagery to a European or American audience such as a young puppy being skinned in a Guangzhou food market. Although the film was attacked by many adoptive parents as one-sided and exaggerated, it simultaneously stimulated others with a missionary spirit to adopt from China.

The HRW/A report was also focused on the neglect of China's orphans in its children's welfare centers. The HRW/A is an international non-profit organization devoted to the amelioration of human rights throughout the world. In its 1996 report, *Death by Default: A Policy of Fatal Neglect in China's State Orphanages*, it purported that the Chinese Government had a national policy, which supported neglect and revilement of its foundlings. It further accused the state children's welfare centers of medical malpractice by the institution's staff, not to speak of the intentional starvation of their charges with the aim of reducing the number of children in the orphanage.

This 331-page report was based much on the statistics furnished by the Chinese Civil Affairs authorities for several

5. Laura A. Cecere, *The Children Can't Wait: China's Emerging Model for Intercountry Adoption* (Cambridge, Mass.: Self-published, 2001), 64.
6. *Ibid.*

provinces in 1989-1990. They indicated that mortality rates in orphanages ranged between 50% and 80%. The medical records smuggled out of the country by Dr. Zhang Shuyun, a doctor at a Shanghai orphanage between 1988-93 were also a contributing factor. Dr. Shuyun claimed that thousands of foundlings were subject to medical neglect as well as starvation with the tactic accord of the government, in particular its senior officials. Dr. Shuyun recounted that there was a tier system whereby the prettiest and the healthiest, in other words the most adoptable, were treated in the better facilities, in this case a downtown orphanage in Shanghai, while the others were sent to a sub-standard welfare center outside the city, the latter a form of hospice. The HRW/A report also underlined that all these institutions should be replaced by foster care, in order to assist the orphans' development; currently finding the system 'needlessly inhuman' with only "a small number of children [saved] from mistreatment and from being starved" through inter-country adoption. The HRW/A also requested that the Chinese allow the orphanages throughout the country to be inspected. The organization filed its report without any direct confrontation with the Chinese authorities because of their "unremitting hostility" to the HRW/A. However, two days after the report was published, surprisingly, twenty journalists from China, England, France, the U.S. and other Western countries were allowed to inspect the Shanghai Children's Welfare Institution, the only orphanage within the city and the one alluded to in the report. They meandered freely throughout the institution's five buildings and engaged in two hours of questions and answers with municipal and orphanage authorities. The reporters concluded that even though the orphanage conditions were poor, with little food, clothing, toys and other amenities, however importantly there were no indication of deliberate starvation or other forms of abuse. One can conclude that, in reality, the orphanage problem was moreover economic and not one of intentional baby genocide. Yet, nonetheless, potential American adopters were very fearful that Washington would impose sanctions on China as a consequence, and placed much pressure on the American Government to avoid such an eventuality.

Simultaneously, the government was aware that the situation with the orphanages was far from optimal. Since 1993, the children's welfare centers have thus profited from a campaign launched by party leader, Jiang Zemin, who is himself an adopted child. His crusade was aimed at assisting foundlings by raising domestic donations and granting free medical care by the local hospitals that formerly charged the orphanages very high prices for their services.

Yet, these improvements notwithstanding, many orphanages, particularly those engaged in foreign adoption have in one way or another been involved in baby trafficking. Generally, this form of corruption has come to have outrageous proportions. Already in 2004, the court convicted fifty-two members of one very large gang for abducting twenty-eight baby girls, none older than three months, who were found in nylon tote bags on a long-distance bus; some of its leaders were given the death sentence and others life imprisonment. Otherwise, child-snatchers have stolen as many as two hundred thousand boys and girls. Fervent adherents of internet, under the guise of adoption, have also sold the stolen youngsters for as much as £ 10,500, each. It is believed that twenty thousand children are snatched annually, that is to say an average of four hundred a week. When they have not been taken away by coercion, fraud or kidnapping, it is sometimes the parents, themselves, who sell their progeny often to avoid being fined for having over-quota children. Some others have also become baby machines claiming that it is more lucrative to sell babies than pigs; babies take only nine months to carry and do not need to be fed versus a pig who takes a year to raise and also needs food. Due to poverty and the country's birth control programs, in rural Yunnan babies are even sold in the marketplace. One seller crying out with enthusiasm: "Come, come. Cheap, cheap. Baby, baby"; two-week-old girls costing on an average the equivalent of $ 25 while their male counterparts, not surprisingly bring the double. This very isolated area near Vietnam houses one of the country's largest underground adoption networks. One gang, alone, smuggled over two thousand babies out of Yunnan in the last five years and sold them to affluent peasants in eastern China who were either childless or in need of extra assistance on their farms and refusing the lengthier wait for legal adoption. As the smugglers search for other children, those who have already been bought or stolen are parked in improvised homes usually under the auspices of very young pre-adolescent girls who have no experience with children, and who accept this work for one dollar a day. When they have gathered a sufficient number, they also take the babies to be sold in the village markets. Afterwards, at nightfall, the traffickers leave with their human cargo in the company of an alleged mother, who is paid $ 35 for her services.

However, not all trafficking is connected to domestic adoption. Children are also kidnapped or allured away from home to be sold into a life on the streets, where they are under the control of adult criminals; they beg and pickpocket and any money the children acquire is taken by the older criminals. Meanwhile, they lie to the youngsters telling them that at least part of the money is being given to their parents. Sometimes teenage boys are also kidnapped and sent to forced labor, or girls are coerced into prostitution.

Yet, probably the most profitable trafficking is when children are sold to orphanages who handle foreign adoption because each foreigner who adopts is obliged to make a $ 5,000 donation in cash in $ 100 bills to the children's welfare center involved; thus, the negotiations between the orphanage and the traffickers occur for much higher stakes. However, government officials are also much too often involved in similar transactions with the orphanages. After forcing parents of out-of-plan children to surrender their offspring to the authorities, the civic officer, himself, sells the child to the orphanage and keeps the proceeds. Often the families are beaten as well as threatened into submitting usually their daughter and manipulated into signing over their parental rights. Furthermore, no government official has ever had the power to take a child away from his parents, so this is another illegal act. One major scandal broke out in 2005 when six orphanages in Hunan, among the largest senders to Western adoption agencies, were tried for baby buying. Although the PRC initially denied the accusation, they later imprisoned a laborer, Duang Yuaneng, and his family who they thought were responsible for trafficking eighty-five infants. As the demand for healthy girls grew, the orphanage paid up to $ 500 per child. The family smuggled in milk powder boxes four infants at a time, on the train between Guangdong to Hunan, a six-hundred-mile train ride. After Duan's prison sentence was terminated, Yuaneng admitted that the number of children involved in the trafficking operation was much closer to a thousand. He reported that thc orphanage also falsified foreign adoption papers for all the children involved. The Chinese Government furthermore claimed that the occurrence in Hunan was an isolated case. However, soon after, a similar scandal occurred. This time family planning officials in Guizhou Province were found to have seized illegally out-of-plan children and sold them to various orphanages; this was reported a few years later in 2009 by the *Los Angeles Times.* Another comparable incident took place two years later when *Caixin*, a news magazine, recounted another such occurrence whereby these children wounded up in American and Dutch families.

Apart from the orphanages, there also exists the SOS Village system to care for orphans and other homeless children. Actually, in China these villages have existed since the mid-1980's when an agreement was signed by the SOS Village charity and the Chinese Ministry of Civil Affairs. As of 1997, there were an increasing number of these SOS Villages throughout China in cities such as Tianjin, Yantai, Qiqihar, Chengdu, Nanchang, Kaifeng and Putian. The charity, at that time, was also planning to create other villages in the Xinjiang Uygur autonomous area as well as the Tibet autonomous region. Orphans were placed in villages of communal homes under the auspices of very carefully selected and trained women, most of whom were unmarried or divorced and had acquired at least a high school if not a university degree. One or two of these women acted in group homes as adoptive mothers for these homeless children. There were usually six to eight children per mother and the children generally range from two to thirteen. Many later found jobs and some even entered university.

A fifteen-year-old girl from the Tianjin SOS Village, who had lost her parents as a child demonstrates the effectiveness of these villages:

> "When I suddenly found that I had a family and asked to call a stranger mama, I could hardly open my mouth." "Now, I love my mother very much. She has done too much for us," said Wei. Wei, the oldest of [her] family group. "I not only have a mother, but also a grandmother and a number of aunts and uncles," she added. "Her mother...has seven brothers and sisters. When holidays and festivals come, the children are taken for family visits and are welcomed by them," she said.[7]

Importantly, it is observed that when these rural children initially enter these communal homes, they are completely unadapted to communal life and furthermore lack even any sense of personal cleanliness. Wei Wei's commentary demonstrates the enormous strides made by these children when they are placed in a nurturing environment. Over the last twenty years the program in China alone has expanded enormously. Today, there are ten SOS Villages and another in Tibet, nine SOS Youth Facilities, ten SOS Kindergartens, one SOS Hermann Greiner School, two Social Centers and two SOS Vocational Training Centers.

Half the Sky, created by Jenny Bower in 1998, is a NGO (non-governmental organization) which works in partnership with the Chinese Government and is in some ways similar to SOS Villages. Like the former, Half the Sky grew tremendously over time and it too commits itself to the needs of orphans and relinquished and disabled children. However, Half the Sky devotes itself entirely to Chinese children and also operates on a much larger scale within the country.

7. *Ibid.*, 73.

As explained in her work *Wish You Happy Forever: What China's Orphans Taught Me About Moving Mountains*, Jenny Bower, a former screenwriter and independent filmmaker, launched Half the Sky as a result of being the adoptive mother of a Chinese daughter who, in a period of months, made such a remarkable transformation from a grief-ridden to an exuberantly happy child that Jenny wanted the same miracle to occur to all the other Chinese baby girls still imprisoned lovelessly in Chinese orphanages. In a period of much sensitivity by the Chinese Government after the numerous orphanage scandals, Bower managed to overcome unimaginable hurdles in order to convince the Communist Party to collaborate with her, a foreigner, to improve orphanage conditions in China. Jenny began her work with two small pilot programs within two children's welfare institutions. Today, in her organization, there are one thousand four hundred and forty staff members who range from caregivers to supervisory program directors. They are currently operating in fifty-three cities and twenty-seven provinces as well as running a medical care home in Beijing, which offers pre- and post-medical services to orphaned babies and young children throughout China who have very serious illnesses. To date, Half the Sky has trained over twenty-eight thousand caretakers and has affected the lives of nearly a hundred and fifty thousand children.

Close to two decades ago, Half the Sky furthermore merged with China's Chanhui Children Program to aid these disadvantaged and marginalized children. Today, they have together four major programs: the Infant Nurture Program, a preschool program, the Little Sisters Preschools Program, a Youth Services Program and a Family Village Program, one resembling in certain respects the SOS Villages Program. In the Infant Nurture Program, babies and toddlers up to three-years-old are cared for by nannies who are retired or laid off workers; they focus on developing emotional bonds with their charges; this early relationship deemed essential for creating later ties of affectivity as well as healthy brain development. Each nanny is responsible for a maximum of four children with whom she sings, plays and cuddles providing all the necessary nurture required by a child of this age. They are also trained to be attuned to any delays occurring in the child's development and are taught the required therapies to overcome any such problems. Afterwards, the Little Sisters Preschools Program consists of a curriculum incorporating the Reggio Emilia approach to early childhood education with the use of current Chinese teaching methods. For these children who are two to seven years old, they are prepared for an academic education as well as a personal one where they are taught a sense of self. Their teachers are at least high school if not university trained and give special attention to each child's interests. They are also required to document each girl's progress. This program additionally prepares them to enter community school where there are other children of the same age group. There are six children to one adult. Meanwhile, the Youth Service Program or Big Sisters Program caters to older children, those from eight to twenty-one-years-old, and provides individual learning possibilities for the girls who have remained in the orphanage and are part of those who are over fourteen and can no longer be adopted. There are ten children to every adult caretaker and as with the younger students, a focus is placed on each girl's individual interests and aptitudes. Almost half of them are accepted in universities and Half the Sky even subsidizes their studies and also gives them vocational training. Apart from their academic development and career training, their personal growth during this period is also strongly emphasized. They are also prepared for living independently through esteem-building mentorship. Otherwise, the Family Village Program is reminiscent of the SOS Villages Program. In the Family Village Program four or five children, this time with special needs, live with a full-time mother and working father in an apartment near or on the orphanage grounds; the parents are usually empty-nest family with grown children. Given the insurmountability of their medical issues, these children have little to no chance of being adopted. Despite their medical conditions, they still, however, attend school and their adoptive mother and father fully commit themselves to them until adulthood.

Finally, through the Rainbow Program floated in 2011, Half the Sky with the collaboration of its Chinese partners is training every child welfare worker throughout the country in order to ameliorate the quality of the care and attention they give to their wards. This program is a government NGO partnership which is financed by the J.P. Morgan Chase Foundation. Otherwise, Half the Sky is funded by individuals and corporate and foundation donors committed to improving the unjustifiable conditions of these outcasts.

Generally, by the turn of the century, the Chinese orphanages were much better subsidized. With the opening of adoption within the country, foreign parents are spending high orphanage fees, at the time $ 3,000, now $ 5,000, as well as making generous donations. Otherwise, the Foundation for Chinese Orphanages sends supplies from medicine to clothes and toys, and also aids financially in foster parent progress as well as medical aid. The Amity Foundation, which is a Christian social service organization, helps numerous orphanages by donating to them a wide range of items from toys to medical provisions. The agency furthermore provides salaries for retired nurses, doctors and teachers in order that they continue to assist the children. The Hayden Foundation additionally finances palate surgeries for orphaned children. UNICEF also helps China in upgrading the state of its orphanages. The Chinese Government, aware of the poor level of some children's welfare institutions, undergoes national fundraising to help improve orphanage conditions.

Initially, transracial adoption to the United States began with the children who were the war victims of WWI. During this period, foreign adoption in America became commonplace and by 1929 every state had an adoption law. Later, after WWII, the U.S. ratified the Displaced Persons Act of 1948 which was the first legislation relating to the immigration of war orphans of WWII. These children were separated from their families and were for the most part adopted by American families.

In 1949, Nobel Prize winner and adoptive mother of seven out of eight children, author Pearl S. Buck was deeply empathetic to the plight of the Asian children who were homeless due to the war. In 1949, she created Welcome Home, the first international and interracial adoption agency in America. The objective was to find parents for children of mixed race whom other such organizations refused to assist. During close to a fifty-year period Welcome Home found parents for close to five thousand children. Buck also supported for a year twelve Chinese children as well as fervently combatting the Chinese Exclusion Acts. Apropos she perceptively remarked: "We send missionaries to China, so the Chinese can get into heaven, but won't let them into our country."[8] When China was taken over by the communists, she went on to assist in adoption from Korea and other parts of Asia. She also established the Pearl S. Buck Foundation for children who were not eligible for adoption as well as the Opportunity Center and Orphanage in South Korea.

Between 1948 and 1962, nearly three thousand Japanese and eight hundred and ten Chinese were adopted once again by white middle class American families; the Japanese adoptions being almost four times higher, probably because the communist government for all intents and purposes, had closed its doors to foreign adoption. Meanwhile, after the end of the Korean War (1950-53), Korea became the lead country in foreign adoptions; there were more than thirty-eight thousand adoptions between 1953 and 1981, when Korea chose to focus instead on domestic ones. However, today total adoptions from Korea are somewhere near a hundred and fifty thousand.

An important player in Korean adoption was an evangelist farmer from Oregon named Harry Holt. After seeing a missionary film about the dilemma of children fathered and then abandoned by American servicemen, Holt opened an orphanage in 1956 in Oregon. He and wife adopted eight Korean children and found homes for another three thousand.

Otherwise, as a consequence of the Refuge Relief Act in 1953 (revoked in 1961) hundreds of children from Japan and China were adopted by proxy and brought to America for adoption. With regards to Korean children, they were viewed as completely

8. Karen Evans, *Lost Daughters of China and the Search for a Missing Past* (N.Y.: Penguin Putnam, 2000), 139.

unadoptable in Korea since children born outside wedlock or of one American and one Korean parent were completely marginalized in their own country; Koreans furthermore placed much emphasis on bloodlines. Thus, inter-country adoption was a means of reducing the potential problems to be faced by a mixed-race child. This notwithstanding, some of the children adopted from Korea as well as Japan and Vietnam during the 1950s and 1960s suffered severe war trauma as well as separation from their birth country and roots. Later, when at least the girls, themselves, became mothers there was a noticeable suicide rate. Otherwise, U.S. adoptions from Vietnam were frequent during the American involvement in the war, but afterwards ended. It was not until the Korean and Vietnam wars that the attention of the Western countries was really focused on children who were orphaned by war, deserted or relinquished by their parents due to the economic or even social consequences of war. Since the 60s the U.S. has increasingly adopted from South and Central America. With the breakup of the Soviet Union and the termination of the Cold War there has been a great increase in inter-country adoption from Russia and former Communist Eastern Europe.

By the 90s, the Chinese Communist Government had a change of heart, but its motivation was probably twofold; on the one hand, the country was overflowing with baby girls and on the other, the government was increasingly accepting contact with the outside world; this being well demonstrated by its Open-Door Policy. Meanwhile, to everyone's astonishment in 1980 an American couple adopted a Chinese infant in China underlining the first inter-country adoption in thirty years by white parents who were not of Chinese descent. The *Washington* Post proclaimed:

> An American couple...have astounded officials [in Beijing] by acquiring a 10-month-old Chinese girl from her poor peasant parents, despite a long time Communist taboo against such adoptions. "Incredible", said a Chinese Foreign Ministry official.... This is China's gift of friendship to America [the administrative judge] said.

> Officials at the U.S. Embassy were so taken aback by the case...that they hesitated to give the baby a visa."[9]

This event was a harbinger of a new era of adoption within China. In 1992, China implemented the first adoption legislation in forty-three years. It formally legalized stranger adoption and importantly recognized the adopted child as equal to the biological one. It also removed the *de facto* stipulation that foreign adoption must be limited to individuals of Chinese ancestry or to those who had worked in China and consequently had added links to the country. It additionally legalized informal adoption, the very common practice of families and friends raising a child instead of his birthparents. Now this child became eligible for a full adoption placing him outside the ambiguous zone of 'black child', one who was unregistered and thus among the many disadvantages was unable to profit from any educational or medical benefits. Additionally, amendments were made in 1999 to the 1992 Adoption Law in order to further encourage the adoption of China's homeless children. The required age for adoption was lowered from over thirty-five to over thirty and childlessness for the adoption of a healthy child was no longer a stipulation. Furthermore, not only disabled and orphaned children were exempt from the One-child policy, but now an exception was also made for abandoned children. One could furthermore adopt more than one disabled, orphaned or abandoned child at a time. It was also during this period that Chinese adoption parents formed groups, called Sunflower Societies, to promote the adoption of the country's parentless children. Since the government approved inter-country adoption in 1992, China has become the principal supplier of international adoptions. The United States is the largest receiving country for Chinese adoptees; with seventy-one thousand six hundred and thirty-two children being assimilated into American families between 1999 and 2013. The U.S. furthermore adopts more Chinese children than any other nation.

---

9. Laura A. Cecere, *The Children Can't Wait: China's Emerging Model for Intercountry Adoption*, 64.

Finally, with regards to adoption the laws differ from one nation to another. Islamic law does not recognize adoption at all, whether domestic or international. In some Eastern and South Asian countries when there is a strong relationship between state and religion, adoption is not acknowledged or foreigners are forbidden to adopt. Kuwait, for instance, being Islamic, has no legal provision for adoption, while Iraq and Qatar do not allow foreign adoption. Israel has very few children available for either domestic or international adoption and when adoption does exist, it is a requisite that children and parents are of the same religion. China and many other Asian countries are more open to adoption because religion is not intrinsically linked to politics; the interrelationship of the two often creating a form of isolation towards other cultures which is reflected also by a nation's attitude and laws relative to adoption. In a similar manner, if a country like China at the time of the communist takeover chose to separate itself from the other nations, this encapsulation, too, has had its impact on adoption.

As mentioned before, Americans adopt more Chinese children than any other nation. The parents are usually white, in their late 30s or early 40s, middle or upper middle class, college educated, professional with relatively high levels of income, living in the suburbs, and are usually childless due to infertility, a state which often leaves them feeling impotent, and in an emotional state reminiscent of their Chinese equivalents. Only 5% of the adoptive parents are single and they are required to sign a paper that they are neither lesbian or gay; the Chinese being particularly sensitive to the issue of homosexuality since until recently it was even found on the list of psychiatric disorders. Furthermore, to qualify for a baby who is around a year old or a younger infant, one must be between the ages of thirty and forty-five, while those between forty-five to fifty can adopt a child between one to three and those between fifty to fifty-five can adopt one between three and six. Only children under fourteen years of age may be adopted and children who are ten or over must also give their consent to the adoption. The Chinese authorities are often hesitant to put older children up for adoption because they fear that the older the child, the greater the problem of adaption; this is particularly true of inter-country adoption where the differences are more apparent on every level. The children, themselves, are also very reluctant to be adopted outside their own country to parents of a different language, culture and race. The older children who have known their birth parents yearn for them to return and bring them home. For those who are visited by relatives, the desire is the same. If not, they hope to be adopted by a family who is as similar as possible to themselves. They in no way aspire to be adopted by a blonde-haired surrogate mother who will whisk them off to America; especially in China, only witches have light hair. Young children who are adopted often cry when they leave the orphanage. They mourn their friends and are concerned about them, often worried that they are not being given enough to eat. Most children who reach pre-adolescence and adolescence remain in the orphanage and become helpers for the caretakers. They are well described by the Chinese born author, Anchee Min:

> They are treated like an eldest child in a family. They know their place and their efforts are appreciated. They grow up emotionally handicapped and don't know it. They have no idea of what affection means, because there are too many children and too few caretakers.[10]

Many Americans turned to inter-country adoption beginning in the 1960s and early 70s because there was a shortage of white babies within the U.S. This was due to the liberalization of abortion laws, the frequent use of contraceptives such as the pill and the condonation of unwed parenthood. Furthermore, in the U.S. according to the Evan B. Donaldson Adoption Institute for every couple who succeeded in adopting a child, there were five or six who did not. The wait for a healthy child was also roughly five years. In addition, the requirements for domestic adoption were more stringent than international adoption. In 1992-95, the process for the adoption of a Chinese child took

10. Karen Evans, *Lost Daughters of China and the Search for a Missing Past,* 164.

only two months or less. In 1995, it was less than six months and now on an average adoption takes one to two years and with little chance of obtaining a completely healthy child because they have already been adopted domestically. Instead, families receive a 'special needs' child; meaning a child with medical and/or developmental problems. 'Special needs' also refers to children over three or four years.

Foreign adopters presently must wait patiently at least five years to adopt a healthy Chinese girl. A healthy boy today is never adopted internationally since when he rarely turns up in a Chinese orphanage, he is automatically given special attention. Apart from the long waiting lists, nearby hotels are packed with peasants waiting to adopt him. Even a moderately disabled or a very sick boy can be very quickly adopted. Older children create another problem. Infants who live in children's welfare centers lose one month of developmental and physical growth for every three or four months they stay in the orphanage. They also incur psychological disorders, infectious diseases and other medical problems. It is also recommended whenever possible that a child is adopted within the first six months in order to later avoid very serious attachment disorder. Many previously contented and extroverted children from six to eleven months become first teary-eyed and introverted, and then completely indifferent to their surroundings. They sit or lie with vacuous eyes and frozen stock-still faces and a ghost-like expression as if they were robots from another planet. Anne F. Thurston very appropriately describes them as miniature versions of the 'Muselmanner' of the Nazi concentration camps; those who were silent, withdrawn and immobile, having given up on life and waiting only for death. René A. Spitz describes the state of these children who spend extensive time institutionalized without any interaction with their mothers as subjects of an 'anaclitic depression'. Bruno Bettelheim refers to them as autistic while the Chinese allude to their condition as "the syndrome of isolation and loneliness".

In China, there are often one foreign adoption for every ten Chinese ones. From 1994 to 1996 and despite China's long reluctancy to stranger adoption, there were still forty thousand domestic adoptions to four thousand inter-country ones. A strongly contributing factor was in all probability the U.N. prioritization of domestic adoption. In 1993, the U.N. Convention on the Rights of the Child stated that:

> Inter-country adoption may be considered as an alternative means of child's care, if the child cannot be placed in a foster or an adoptive family or cannot in any suitable manner be cared for in the child's country of origin.[11]

For foreign adoption, the adoption process operates as follows: parents choose an adoption agency in America as an example and take care of the required paperwork for the agency and the American and Chinese Government. Sometimes, the families also receive pre-adoption training. Simultaneously, orphanages having children eligible for adoption send "referrals" to the China Center of Adoption Affairs, the CCAA, in Beijing. Some of the children who are recommended are issue of small to large orphanages as well as foster care. Once the parents' pre-adoption paperwork is complete, including an application for the child's visa, the file is sent to the CCAA for approval. At this point parents are rather arbitrarily matched with a child and sent a small photograph and, when uncertain, an estimated guess of the child's date of birth and some other critical information such as her height, weight, medical history as well as a name given by the orphanage. Girls' names are often generic (Xiao Mei, Little Sister), while names for boys are much more personalized for evident reasons. Otherwise, children arriving in the same month are all given an identical surname (January, February, March...).

Furthermore, prior to adoption those who are not already in foster care are usually placed there so they can benefit from a more nurturing and humanized environment in preparation for their adoption. After at least a year's wait, the parents are then approved for travel to China which usually requires a two-week period with other administrative paperwork, and most

11. Laura A. Cecere, *The Children Can't Wait: China's Emerging Model for Intercountry Adoption*, 127.

importantly, collecting their adopted progeny. Their journey also involves a stop to Shamian Island where the American consulate processes adoption visas necessary for the family's departure. In the past, many adopting families parked themselves at Shamian's five-star hotel, the White Swan Hotel, otherwise dubbed the White Stork Hotel. Until recently when most of the adopting families have moved to the China Hotel, the White Swan Hotel became a type of baby boarding house. This glass multistory hotel overlooking the Pearl River assigned three floors with all the amenities necessary for these newly composed families. Each family also received a limited-edition Mattel doll named "Going Home Barbie", a blonde Barbie doll clasping a Chinese baby; today these dolls cost $ 300. Shamian Island is filled with shops catering to the needs of the parents and their newly adopted offspring. One can find stores selling pink and red silk Chinese baby dresses to artists drawing portraits of the newly adopted babies. Before leaving Guangdong, foreign adopting parents today have usually spent over $ 30,000 including travel and hotel and adoption expenses, comprising, of course, the $ 5,000 donation to the orphanage. Meanwhile, domestic adoption can also be the same amount or can vary drastically being twenty to thirty times less and at other times determined simply by the family's income. Some children's welfare centers, when the staff is not walking off with toys, furniture and other gifts to the orphanage or the head of the orphanage has not pocketed enough money to send his daughter to school in Switzerland, are also known to inform Chinese adopters that there are no appropriate children for them, in order to guarantee for themselves the higher fee required by foreigners.

Although most Americans are unable to adopt the White American dream baby, many are very reluctant to adopt an African-American child because while an Asian child can 'pass', a black child cannot. Significantly, too, while Asian Americans are the 'model minority', blacks instead are associated inversely with thanklessness, welfare dependency and even criminality. Black women also have poor prenatal care and during pregnancy often smoke, drink and take drugs being infamous for their 'crack' babies; the Chinese women, by contrast, are renowned for their sobriety, not indulging in any of these 'vices'. The United States, furthermore, has much more open adoption politics than any other nation and many adopting parents do not want contact with the birthmother or worse yet, they fear she might attempt to reclaim the child. In China, the child's custody has been transferred to the orphanage and by the time of adoption, the rights of the birthmother are already terminated, which naturally is reassuring to the child's future adoptive parents.

Otherwise, Russia and other former Eastern European Communist countries are often another option which is initially appealing, given the children are Caucasian. However, the drawbacks soon outweigh the advantages. The government's corruption in these countries, especially in Romania, with regards to their adoption practices has discouraged many foreign adopters. These children are also more neglected, institutionalized longer and are not placed in foster care prior to adoption as their Chinese counterparts. They also have multiple caretakers and have limited contact with others. Thus, they almost inevitably have severe attachment disorders. Consequently, they are subject to retarded social-behavioral, cognitive, affective and conscience development. They are handicapped in making friendships and accepting responsibility. Like the African Americans, they have also received poor to no prenatal care and like the American blacks often have mothers dependent on alcohol, drugs and cigarettes.

The Chinese have received more favorable prenatal care as well as pre-adoptive experiences, including relatively better care in the orphanages. Many have importantly had a continuous relationship with caregivers unlike the other adoptees. Thus, they are much more capable of attachment to their adopted mother and family; they are therefore viewed as better candidates for adoption. Chinese children are also considered to have easier temperaments than Caucasian children, not to speak of Black ones. They are also lauded in America for their beauty, intelligence, sprightliness, musicality and diligence, they are alleged to even surpass their white counterparts.

However, with all this being said, they also share with all adopted children the loss of the biological parents as well as added losses such as the separation from their pre-adoption caretakers and from their country of birth and culture. In general adoptees receive two to five times as much psychological or psychiatric counseling than biological children, most of their problems being generated once again by loss. Psychological studies have shown that in the six to eleven age range for instance, the adoptees are more inclined towards psychological and school related behavioral problems. Their social skills and school marks are usually lower than non-adopted children. It has been observed that they have higher rates of academic problems, learning disabilities, attention deficit, and hyperactivity disorders. Male children are also more subject to these problems than females. This could be true because a boy may be more in need of roots than a girl who through her situation needs to be more flexible and adaptable. Additionally, a minority adoptee raised in a non-minority family often also has low self-esteem and insufficient racial identity. This is why it is important for the child to be rooted in her culture; contact with other Chinese children, such as enrolling her in playgroups with them, language lessons and sometimes even a bilingual school and celebration of important Chinese holidays such as the Red Lantern Festival or Chinese New Year are all aids in helping her identify and take pride in her heritage. As she gets older, some families take her to China and back to the place she was found and the orphanage in which she lived. For most of these girls this is a very healing experience allowing them to create a sense of self and a sense of wholeness; for some, however, it can result in a very disruptive experience where even though some questions are answered even more remain unanswered.

In any case, those children who are told at a very earlier age as recommended go through the same stages as the ones attributed to the Indian children. These phases are, in fact, universal that is initially fantasizing about the birthmother, to becoming curious about the birthmother, to feeling the loss related to the adoption, followed by the hurt and anger. By the time the Chinese child reaches adolescence the issues of identity also become a problem and an area of focus. Somewhere one can come to question whether it is better that a child learns about the adoption, particularly when there are no physical differences between the adoptee and the adoptive family. Yet, the worst scenario and one where he inevitably feels the most betrayed is when he learns about his past through a third party and sometimes completely inadvertently.

Otherwise, for the Chinese adoptees, there is a sophisticated and most efficacious service which was created by an ex-Mormon, Brian Stuy, who is also the adoptive father of three Chinese daughters. In 2004, he and his Chinese wife floated a small company, Research China, whereby they collected finding advertisements for which they paid a few cents and resold them to adoptive parents for $ 75 each. Orphanages are required to publish these advertisements for all children who are programmed for foreign adoption. Through Research China, many adoptive parents were able to acquire additional information with regards to their adopted child. Soon after, they extended their company to include customized reports on specific orphanages, using information from the finding ads. They studied the six Hunan orphanages as well as other state child welfare centers, concluding that a majority of orphanages have been involved in baby buying; shocking news to good Samaritan adoptive families. Furthermore, only four years ago they began birth parent searches using DNA testing. They first located an orphanage known for trafficking children and afterwards contacted a group of parents having adopted from the same orphanage. Next, the Stuys initiated a search which involved interviews with foster parents and orphanage workers in the area and gathered DNA samples. Adoptive parents pay $ 275 as a deposit and if the birth parents are found pay another $ 200.

It is important also to understand the historical racism faced by the Chinese as well as other Asians for over a hundred and fifty years in the United States. Given that the majority of these Chinese girls have been adopted in the States, one must underline that in the land of liberty, where America's 1790 Naturalization Law only allowed 'free white persons' to become citizens, the Chinese have probably been the ethnic group, along with the Japanese, the most reviled; otherwise, sometimes worse yet, they have simply been invisible, in other words treated as non-existent. In fact, by the 1960s, the overt racism which they endured gradually became more covert, barring a few exceptions. Adopted Chinese children and their families are still often victims of some form of racism, much stemming from the earlier prejudices and negative stereotypes that were attributed to their Chinese forefathers.

During the mid-nineteenth century great numbers of Chinese immigrated to America as indentured servants at the time of the California Gold Rush. As early as 1859, the California State legislative made it illegal for Negroes, Mongolians and Indians to be admitted in the public schools. After the Civil War, when African-Americans were given citizenship, naturalization was denied the Chinese; this was justified by the fact that they were neither white nor black. By the late 1870s, the anti-Chinese "Yellow Peril" movement seized the West. Riots against the Chinese erupted throughout that part of the country. Murders and lynchings were far-reaching. Homes, shops and laundries as well as barns and fields were burned. This unceasing racism against them culminated in 1882 with the Chinese Exclusion Act, which prohibited Chinese immigration and also barred legal residents from becoming citizens. The twentieth century opened with California passing a law whereby 'aliens ineligible to citizenship' were prevented from buying land or leasing it for over three years; a law most deleterious for the Chinese farmers.

However, the worst backlash against Chinese Americans began in the 1950s as a reaction to the communist threat, while plane loads of China's relinquished babies, toddlers and young girls were arriving in the country accompanied by their adoptive parents, America was in a state of paranoia that the generation of their abandoning parents, even their grandparents, were spying against the United States, the country ironically adopting their deserted children. "The Red Menace" created virulent racism against the Chinese, which could include by extension even the Chinese adopted children and their adoptive American parents, not to speak of the country's Chinese population at large. The Chinese Americans and probably even some of these adoptive parents were riddled with fear that they, too, might be relegated to internment camps as were the Japanese Americans a decade earlier. For at least the Chinese Americans, their terror became a self-fulfilling prophecy because in 1950 Congress passed a bill, the McCarran Internal Security Act, whereby an individual suspected of espionage on reasonable grounds was to be imprisoned. In Chinatown, signs were even posted in Chinese, announcing the existence of a "Confession Program" in which Chinese Americans were induced to report on friends and relatives who were thought to be spying. In return, they were granted legal immigration status; in San Francisco alone ten thousand people partook. In 1969, Edgar Hoover, director of the FBI, furthermore cautioned his countrymen that:

> The United States is Communist China's No. 1 enemy. Red China has been flooding the country with propaganda and there are over 300,000 Chinese in the United States, some of them who could be susceptible to recruitment either through ethnic ties or hostage situations because of relatives in Communist China.[12]

Yet, during the 1960s, Americans had a dual stance in relation to the Chinese. On the one hand, they were still feared as a Communist menace, but on the other hand, being Asian, they had become part of the "model minority" and were admired for their industriousness and their achievements. Their image being well synthesized in a 1966 article in the *U.S. News World Report* which publicized an article entitled "Success Story of One Minority Group in the United States", eulogizing them and contrasting them to African Americans:

---

12. M. Evelina Galang, ed. *Screaming Monkeys: Critiques of Asian American Images* (Minneapolis, Minn.: Coffee House Press, 2001), 116.

> At a time when Americans are awash in worry over the plight of racial minorities, one such minority, the nation's 300,000 Chinese Americans, is winning wealth and respect by dint of its own hard work.... Still being taught in Chinatown is the old idea that people should depend on their own efforts – not a welfare check-in order to reach America's 'Promised Land'.[13]

In fact, the positive representation of the Chinese was in large part due to the more than problematic, disruptive and hostile position of the American Negro at that time.

Historically, the Chinese had been viewed as the 'inscrutable alien enemy'. They were alluded to as 'Chinks', 'Chinamen' or 'Yellow lepers' and considered as dirty, uncivilized, immoral, criminal and by some even as borderline humans. The women were simply perceived as prostitutes. The Chinese were also perceived as 'opium-sodden' and filled with 'treacherous mendacity' and 'heathenish ways'. However, by the mid to late 60s, America was faced with a new foe, the Black Power Movement, which was a far cry from the earlier Civil Rights Movement headed by Martin Luther King. While the initial movement stressed passive resistance as the means by which African Americans could achieve their goals of equality and integration, Black Power focused on violent, militant action to reach the same ends. White America, from Newark to Los Angeles trembled as these angry blacks rioted and looted from one end of the country to the other. Their tempestuous attitude was well summarized by the notorious American writer Norman Mailer, when he stated in *Cannibals and Christians* that "the militant black left...swear whitey must eat turd before peace is here."[14] Their vehemence was also manifested by the National Association of Black Social Workers [NABSW] created in 1968. The NABSW protested against transracial adoption placements, especially the adoption of Negro children by white families. For

---

13. M. Evelina Galang, ed. *Screaming Monkeys: Critiques of Asian American Images*, 117-18.
14. Norman Mailer, *Cannibals and Christians* (N.Y.: Dial Press, 1966), 61.

them, this was the ultimate manifestation of "race genocide". Thus, laws have even been passed in order that the adopting white parents will not be discriminated against as a consequence of race. Yet, in some cases, these prospective parents still report that they nevertheless suffer from reverse discrimination in their attempt to adopt a child who is black or bi-racial.

Concurrently, the Chinese and other Asian Americans were influenced by the Negro in the sense that they grew to have more racial pride, self-esteem and self-assertion as a consequence. During this period, without at all the same anger or violence, they in their turn enthusiastically identified themselves with "Yellow Power"; not only was "Black Beautiful", but now Yellow had also become beautiful. Some university students promoted the education of Asian history in American colleges, others went on strike against the U.S. invasion of Asian countries, whether Vietnam or Cambodia, while still others became lawyers and took the defense of fellow Asian Americans who were the victims of discrimination.

It is understandable how in this stormy racial climate that the Asians and specifically the Chinese grew to be esteemed, but it has nonetheless been an ongoing struggle and continues. Otherwise, legislation is often one of the best barometers of a country's attitude towards race. While in 1943 a handful of Chinese were granted citizenship, by 1965 the National Origins Act raised immigration to twenty thousand people per year for Asian countries, which was the same quota allowed for European nations. Meanwhile, by 1956 Dalip Singh Sound, an Asian Indian was the first Asian American elected to Congress, followed in 1964 by Patsy Takemoto Mink, who was the first Asian American elected to the House of Representatives. Afterwards, in 1996 Gary Locke, still another individual of Asian background, became the first Governor of the State of Washington. Consequently, one can conclude that white America was slowly but surely permitting the integration of the once 'inscrutable alien enemy'. Asian immigration furthermore soared from over 850,000 in 1960 to 7.3 million in 1990; they are now the fastest growing minority in the United States and thus, by their presence alone have surpassed their former invisibility.

This notwithstanding, prejudice and discrimination against the Chinese and other Asian ethnic groups is still present today and is an undeniable element in any transracial adoption. Its pertinence is well analyzed by the author, Jana Wolff, in *Secret Thoughts of an Adoptive Mother*, herself mother of an adopted child who is a combination of African-American, Latino and white:

> Back in our pre-adoption "Dark Ages", I thought race was a non-issue when it came to parenting. In fact, it is the issue. We have to deal with race before adoption, because it is more immediately noticeable to other people. I've evolved from an unenlightened white woman who thought all people should be treated equally, to an enlightened one who knows they are not....[15]

Gail Steinberg, one of the directors of Pact, An Adoption Alliance and the adoptive mother of four children who are Korean, African-American, Caucasian and bi-racial, confirms the importance of racism in racial adoption. She further focuses on the need to educate these children in order to cope with the inevitable prejudice and discrimination which they will necessarily encounter: "The important things they have taught me is how much race matters.... If I could go back and be a better parent, I would do as much as I could to prepare – not protect – them."[16] Author and adoptive mother, Cheri Register, also concurs that race is key in these adoptions and focuses on the unconsciousness of whites in regard to race. Since a white individual is not a victim of racial discrimination, Register implies that he is unable to identify with or comprehend its victims. Apropos of race related to transracial adoption, she states:

> I never suspected it to pervade my life and consciousness the way it has. But as the result of having my daughters,

15. Myra Alperson, *Dim Sum, Bagels and Grits: A Sourcebook for Multicultural Families* (N.Y.: Farrar, Straus and Giroux, 2001), 55.
16. *Ibid.*, 47.

> it has become a really important subject for me to explore – to look at "whiteness" as race and how much is taken for granted.[17]

Thus, these parents are aware that apartheid and discrimination pervade the lives of their families. Not only are the parents, themselves, affected, but most importantly these Chinese girls become the targets of bigotry even as small children. Some families decide to change neighborhoods and move to a more mixed community so they, themselves, and particularly their adopted children, have the possibility of being assimilated, a crucial factor for their girls' identity and self-esteem. Differentness, uniqueness is a condition which is furthermore accepted with difficulty in many conservative areas of white, puritanical America.

The issue of personal integration is further intensified when the adoptee enters a family that already includes biological children. By comparison, especially as she grows older, she can come to feel alienated and unable to identify herself as a member of the family. These Chinese girls also not being of the same race nor ethnic group as their adoptive parents have a driving need for acceptation. These children are doubly sensitive to the issue of assimilation since they are both adopted and Mongolian, neither white nor black. Their otherness often makes them feel like outsiders. Some feel a certain hostility directed towards themselves as early as when they first attend kindergarten. Much of this prejudice can be attributed to color differences and especially a diverse physical appearance, which make these children stand out against the majority of their white peers, particularly their schoolmates. Thus, they are frequently ridiculed and humiliated and treated as inferior by their contemporaries; children often being terribly conformist and threatened by any form of diversity. Also, their biological parents are another contributing factor, as they often transmit to them the negative stereotypes, which they themselves have made credible for decades. As the Chinese girl, for instance, reaches adolescence she has frequently integrated these negative

---

17. *Ibid.*, 146.

stereotypes. These "Yellow Lepers", these "Chinks" are not only physically different, but are perceived by the others as also dissimilar in mentality; importantly, these girls too have come to view themselves as distinct or subordinate to their seemingly superior white peers. Puberty anyway, is a very fragile time. For these vulnerable adolescents the loss of the birthmother becomes especially dolorous. This applies to girls more than boys because being a female the girl identifies more with the mother.

Otherwise, the later a girl is adopted, the greater the problems of assimilation. As an older girl not only does she continues to look differently, but the older she is the more baggage she brings with her. She recalls her past life; sometimes within her biological family and if not, certainly within the orphanage. In some cases, too, she remembers her abandonment, which is considered the most grievous moment in a Chinese girl's life. She furthermore has assimilated some Chinese culture and, worse yet, can communicate only in her own language. In these cases, the adoptive family is recommended to submerge her into the Chinese American community and to expose her to everything Chinese to facilitate her transition. It is also advocated that the adoptive parents maintain her original name in order to diminish any further complications relating to her identity. This is additionally a means by which she can take pride in her Chinese selfhood and strengthen herself against any potential discrimination. However, interestingly it is the girl, herself, who usually wishes to relinquish her name which is synonymous with her former identity and her past, which tends to be extremely painful. Some Chinese girls even remember their orphanage lives, reporting their recollection of being less than a year old and tied to orphanage beds or potty chairs. Consequently, their only desire is to forget their past and to become assimilated into a better world. This explains the rapidity with which they can acquire a new language such as English and just as quickly forget the old one.

The Asian American woman's need to integrate occurs almost systematically. Those who are adopted experience the same desire, but only more intensely as by definition they are more marginalized and therefore more vulnerable. Generally, Asian American adolescents, for instance, disclose an impartial to an even derogatory opinion about their own racial group. Their yearning for assimilation is notably higher than other ethnic groups such as the Hispanics or African Americans. Even though the Chinese American female is known to be more involved in her Chinese roots than other transracial adoptees, she nonetheless not only seeks assimilation, but if she could choose, she like her Asian American sisters, would almost inevitably prefer to be white. The great majority of her friends are white, as are the men she dates and marries. She chooses Caucasian men because she has integrated the belief that whites are superior. Her attitude furthermore shows a certain similitude to the one portrayed by the Caribbean writer and psychiatrist Franz Fanon in *Black Skin, White Masks*. Here, he claims that a black man who systematically has sex with white women has the fallacy that his feelings of inferiority will be eradicated through the sexual act. The Asian American woman, particularly the adoptee, seeks also through sexual intimacy a certain form of osmosis. Given the prejudice she is forced to undergo, she, too, becomes very concerned with her physical appearance. Intermarriage, for many of these women, particularly adoptees, is also a means of rejecting their own negative body image; the importance attributed to their small stature, yellow skin, slit almond eyes, flat nose and short legs tends to disappear, or at least diminish, when they become the wife of their opposite, that tall, blue eyed, blond haired WASP (White Anglo Saxon Protestant). However, publicly, she justifies her choice by stating that she has little to no contact with Asian men where she lives, that they are physically unattractive or that they are too traditional and would find her too Western. She always maintains that she married for love and insists that her emotions are completely color blind, which most of the time is probably not the case.

American Chinese women are no longer perceived as prostitutes, but instead exotic, sensual and submissive. Their male equivalent, however, is seen as effeminate and not appealing by American standards. While the women are frequently candidates for intermarriage, the Chinese American male is much more hesitant due to the Chinese tradition of patriarchy. He is often concerned that, should he return to China, he might encounter some form of exclusion with a foreign wife.

When the parents, themselves, are Chinese and not white, the Chinese daughter, and especially the adopted daughter, is faced with another set of problems. Since the value system in China and in the United States is totally antithetical, parents and children are often in conflict. These issues are once again only magnified for the adoptee. The Chinese maintain that an individual must contain his emotions while an American feels that feelings should be expressed. Chinese society is collective, and the family is of paramount importance and the individual is little taken into consideration. Even the obsessive attention placed on achievement is not perceived as an individual accomplishment but as a family one. Chinese society focuses on the parents and not the children, obedience to elders, filial piety[18] and duty, not love, is paramount. In American society, when a child reaches adulthood, if not even earlier, he is deemed to be equal to his parents; in China he is always subordinated. Finally, and importantly is the Asian belief in male superiority, instead of once again of male-female equality. In a word, "Traditional Asian families are run more like monarchies than democracies."[19]

The conflicts faced by an Asian American woman are well expressed by the Chinese American author, Claire S. Chow in *Leaving Deep Water: The Lives of Asian American Women at the Crossroads of Two Cultures.* In the preface, she confesses the limbo in which she lives:

---

18. Even cannibalism is an act of filial piety. Records from the Song dynasty relate how an individual would cut off part of his own body to feed a venerated elder. Until the government issued an edit against it, a daughter-in-law would cut flesh from her leg or thigh to make soup for an ill mother-in-law.
19. Claire S. Chow, *Leaving Deep Waters: The Lives of Asian American Women at the Crossroads of Two Cultures* (N.Y.: Penguin Books, 1998), xii-xiii.

> What, then, does it mean to be Asian American? To me, it means living in a place where I don't look much like anyone else but in most respects act like them, knowing all the time that halfway across the globe is a densely populated region full of people who look just like me. It means forever holding the contradiction of belonging and not belonging, of feeling "at home" and wondering where home is. It means living with other people's ideas about me, ideas that often do not coincide with the person I really am. It means doubting my self-concept. It means occasionally still wishing I was white. It means occasionally still feeling the sting of shame about my ethnicity trickling out from hidden places. It means wishing, just this once, that someone could step into my shoes and see what life is like from my perspective... Aware that it is up to me to define my life and my identity because in the end, I am the one who must live with the consequences of all these contradictions.[20]

In her book, the author further laments her mongrel status and clearly states the difficulty she finds in finding her own identity: "I don't feel fully American or fully Chinese. I am some kind of strange new hybrid and I have to make my own way. I have to decide what being Asian American means to *me*."[21] One Korean adoptee further expounds on the problem of being biracial and concludes that it can only be resolved when an individual chooses one of the two cultures: "Being a Korean adoptee puts you in 'Never Never Land' until you make a commitment to either side. You are not white, and you are not Korean."[22]

Adoption is rarely a first choice and almost inevitably involves loss at one level or another; for the adopting parent the sense of loss involved in infertility, for the adoptee the loss of birthparents and pre-adoption caretakers. The complexity of adoption is augmented through interracial and inter-country

20. *Ibid.*, 190-91.
21. *Ibid.*
22. Myra Alperson, *Dim Sum, Bagels and Grits: A Sourcebook for Multicultural Families*, 27.

adoption in the sense that the differences between adoptee and adopting parents are more apparent and overtime the problem of identity for the adoptee is greatly increased. Consequently, today China as most developing countries, like India, prioritizes domestic over international adoption and in fact remains very ambivalent toward inter-country adoption. On the other hand, foreign adoption is much more lucrative but on the other is humiliating because it supposes that China as well as the other third world countries are unable to adequately provide for their children. Thus, despite China's seven hundred thousand homeless children, out of a sense of inferiority, some Chinese defensively perceive adoption as "a new form of colonialism, with wealthy Westerners robbing poor countries of their children and their resources."[23]

23. Jay W. Rojewski and Jacy L. Rojewski, *Intercountry Adoption from China: Examining Cultural Heritage and Other Postadoption Issues* (Westport, Conn. and London: Bergin & Garvey, 2001), 22.

Conclusion

> Will you know, the biggest question for me is how does she deal with the fact that her birth mother gave her up – her birth parents. How do you explain that? Now you can say to her well they did it because they wanted a boy. Well, I don't think that's gonna go over too well.
>
> … The truth of the matter is, people in China and India give up their kids because they want boys! They give up their girls. That's the reality and at some point, we're gonna have to tell her that.[1]
>
> *Aaron Kretz, adoptive father*

Patriarchy and the practice of gender discrimination is deeply ingrained and more widespread in the developing countries of Asia and Africa than in the developed countries of the West. This phenomena exists throughout the females' lifespan and is particularly evident during childhood, the latter part of the reproductive system and old age. Daughters who are the offspring of families having more than one daughter are moreover the victims of misogyny than those girls who are children in one-child families who manage to escape at least in part the problem of misogyny. The infant mortality rate and the maternal mortality rate are both higher in India than in China. A woman's life expectancy is longer, and her general health status is also much better in China. The Chinese are

1. Sara K. Dorow, *Transnational Adoption: A Cultural Economy of Race, Gender, and Kinship* (N.Y. and London: New York University Press, 2006), 175.

more familiar and adept regarding birth control, and even despite the One-child or even the Two-child policy, are rarely conditioned to having the very large families so often common in India. Furthermore, the marriage age in China is twenty-three versus eighteen and in Muslim communities even less in India. Thus, this is another factor which adds to the Indian woman's vulnerability. In old age, the Chinese woman also does not face the prejudice so often still attached to widowhood as does her Indian counterpart. Particularly in urban areas, she also often enjoys a minimum of social security such as rent-free housing, some pension, free medical aid, institutionalized rehabilitation or support as well as free burial expenses, all of which are still unheard of in India.

Otherwise, economics, education and religion are fundamental in understanding some of the differences between the two countries. Despite a certain extremely wealthy elite, India is a much poorer nation than China where the income levels of the destitute are so minimal that many of the poor are still unable to afford even the most basic necessities such as a minimal amount of food, schooling, hospitalization or sanitation facilities, even lacking a toilet in their homes when they are not simply living in the streets. Even today as many as half of all Indians are forced to resort to the open defecation so castigated by V.S. Naipaul, while in China only 1% of the population find themselves relegated to this atrocious poverty. China, by contrast, unlike India, devotes twice as much of its public revenue to services such as education, health and nutrition.

Likewise, even though India may boast of having the highest enrollment in foreign universities and proudly claims to produce the greatest number of engineers and other highly skilled professionals, these are still only part of the happy few, given that simultaneously India has the highest rate of illiteracy worldwide; one-fourth of Indian men and almost one-half of Indian women are illiterate. Rabindranath Tagore appropriately concluded that "the imposing load of misery which rests on the heart of India has its 50% foundation in the absence of education."[2] Currently, in China, women in relationship to men have come to be on an equal footing at the level of education and even consist of a majority of the country's workforce.

Religion is the other important dissimilarity marking the two countries. While China is predominantly Buddhist, the majority of Indians are Hindu. While Buddhism stresses equality, Hinduism focuses on inequality. Although both believe in *karma*, Hinduism, unlike Buddhism, underlines the inferiority of women which is justified as a consequence of their *karma*. Furthermore, the emphasis on Buddhism or Christianity is on the responsibility to the community versus the accent in Hinduism is placed only on one's personal salvation. After examining the differences in economics, education, and religion one comes to understand why China is in advance of India and why it will probably continue to supersede it in dealing with the problems of gender imbalance due to both nations' adherence to patriarchal values.

Even though China has better surmounted Asia's patriarchal system, it nevertheless remains detrimental to both countries. Women have for centuries been treated like second class citizens. The male has instead been venerated as he has been responsible for the family's material and spiritual well-being. Consequently, the female has suffered from rampant feticide, infanticide, and abandonment resulting at best in her adoption, whether locally or abroad. The rise in the "disappearance" of girls in both countries has enacted an imbalanced sex-ratio which neither India nor China are able to assume. As synthesized in April, 2018 by "The Nation", one of Bangkok's leading newspapers, that there are "just too many men: China and India grapple with consequences of societies with too many males, leading to social consequences."[3] Men in both nations are desperately searching for mates resorting to all sorts of stratagems from human-size blow-up dolls, illegal immigration of females or simply buying a woman, even a wife. Richard Saltus has perceptively added:

2. Jean Drèze and Amartya Sen, *An Uncertain Glory and Its Contradictions* (New Delhi: Allen Lane, 2013), 107.
3. *The Nation*, April 28, 2018, p. 4A.

"What triggers most wars is not ideology or honor but a society bottom-heavy with young unmarried and violent-prone males...one country where conditions may be brewing trouble is China."[4] Of course, the same may be said for India. Yet, in fact in both countries, schemes have been created to enhance the value of the girl child whereby families are encouraged not to kill or desert their baby girls but instead to protect and nourish them in order that they will become the country's future wives and mothers.

In recent years, many of these infant girls have been abandoned, surrendered or stolen for adoption. They have since become a commodity particularly in Western countries where fertility has been on the decline. Even though historically stranger adoption is not part of Asian culture, it is gradually becoming more acceptable. Yet, after the numerous scandals in both countries, China has become extremely closed with regards to foreigners visiting its orphanages, while India remains completely open, welcoming, and transparent in relation to the occasional presence of outsiders within their children's welfare centers. Even though officially there are ten times more adoptions either locally or internationally in China, in both countries and particularly in India many infants and young children are laundered, and adoption has become a major corruption-ridden industry. Adoption is basically a painful price for both the adoptive parent and the adoptee, both the inevitable products of loss. As concluded by author, Emily Buchanan: "One of the inescapable truths about adoption is that when you adopt, you are also adopting the world's pain. You can't live in a bubble and pretend bad things don't happen."[5] With the current situation the anguish is only increasing. When embassy staff recently sent over a thousand children abroad and were asked which adoption visas they felt uneasy about, they replied 'almost all of them'. As resumed by David Smolin:

---

4. Karen Evans, *Lost Daughters of China and the Search for a Missing Past* (N.Y.: Penguin Putnam, 2000).
5. Emily Buchanan, *From China With Love: A Long Road to Motherhood* (West Sussex: John Wiley & Sons, 2005), 167.

> Unless we recognize that behind the altruistic veneer, international adoption has become an industry – one that is often highly lucrative and sometimes corrupt – many more adoption stories will have unhappy endings...credulous Westerners eager to believe that they are saving children are easily fooled into accepting laundered children.... For there is no fool like the one who wants to be fooled.[6]

6. E.J. Graff, "The Lie We Love", *Foreign Policy* (November/December 2008), 66.

Bibliography

Allen, Michael and Mukherjee, eds. *Women in India and Nepal*, Canberra, Australia: ANU Printing for the South Asian History Section of the Australian National University, Canberra, 1982, 252.

Ahmad, Imtiaz, "Adoption in India: A Study of Attitudes." *The India Review of Social Work*, 36, No. 2 (July, 1975): 181-90.

Aird, John S. *Coercive Birth Control in China*. Lanham, Md. and London: AEI Press, 2006.

Akbar, M.J. *Nehru: The Making of India*. New Delhi: Roli Books Pvt. Ltd., 2002.

Alperson, Myra. *Dim Sun, Bagels and Grits: A Sourcebook for Multicultural Families*. N.Y.: Farrar, Straus and Giroux, 2001.

Altekar, A.S. *Position of Women in Hindu Civilization*. New Delhi: Motilal Banarsidass, 1959, 252.

Andersen, M.D. Robert. *Second Choice: Growing Up Adopted*. Chesterfield, Mo.: Badger Hill Press, 1993.

Bales, Kevin. *Disposable People*. Berkeley: University of California Press, 2012.

Bajpai, Asha. *Adoption and Justice to the Child*. Bangalore, India: National Law School of India University, 1996.

Bharat, Shalini. *Child Adoption: Trends and Emerging Issues (A Study of Adoption Agencies)*. Bombay: Tata Institute of Social Sciences, 1993.

Bhargava, Vinita. *Adoption in India: Policies and Experiences.* New Delhi, Thousand Oaks, California and London: Sage Publications, 2005.

Billimoria, H.M. *Child Adoption—A Study of Indian Experience.* Bombay: Himalaya Publishing House, 1984.

Bower, Jenny. *Wish You Happy Forever: What China's Orphans Taught Me About Moving Mountains.* N.Y.: Harper Collins, 2014.

Bright, Jagat Singh, ed. *Important Speeches of Jawaharlal Nehru. A Collection of Most Significant Speeches Delivered by Jawaharlal Nehru from 1922-1945.* Lahore: The Indian Printing Works, 1945.

Brodzinsky, D.M. and Schechter, M.D., eds. *Being Adopted: The Lifelong Search for Self.* N.Y.: Doubleday, 1992.

Buchanan, Emily. *From China With Love: A Long Road to Motherhood.* West Sussex, England: John Wiley & Sons, 2005.

Bumiller, Elisabeth. *May You be the Mother of a Hundred Sons: A Journey Among the Women of India.* N.Y.: Fawcett Columbine, 1990.

Caplan, Patricia. *Class and Gender in India: Women and their Organizations in a South Indian City.* London and N.Y.: Tavistock Publications, 1985.

Carney, Scott. *The Red Market: On the Trail of the World's Organ Brokers, Bone Thieves, Blood Farmers, and Child Traffickers.* N.Y.: William Morrow, 2011.

Cecere, Laura A. *The Children Can't Wait: China's Emerging Model for Intercountry Adoption.* Cambridge: Mass.: Self-published, 2001.

Chang, Pang-Mei Natasha. *Bound Feet & Western Dress.* N.Y.: Random House, 1997.

Choudary, Kirti. *Women and Fertility Behavior.* Jaipur: Pointer Publishers, 2012.

Chaudhuri, Nirad C. *Hinduism: A Religion to Live by.* N.Y.: Oxford University Press, 1979.

Child Adoption and Thereafter: A Psycho Analytical Study. Tamil Nadu: Indian Council for Child Welfare, Tamil Nadu, 2001.

China's Children: Adoption, Orphanages, And Children With Disabilities. Washington D.C.: U.S. Government Printing Office, 2003.

Chow, Claire S. *Leaving Deep Waters: The Lives of Asian American Women at the Crossroads of Two Cultures.* N.Y.: Penguin Books, 1998.

Clark, E. Andrey and Hanisee, Jeanette. "Intellectual and Adoptive Performance of Asian Children in Adoptive American Settings". *Developmental Psychology,* 18, No. 4 (1982): 595-99.

Cowasjee, Saros and Duggal, K.S., eds. *Orphans of the Storm: Stories of the Partition of India.* New Delhi: UBS Publishers & Distributors Ltd., 1995.

Das, Gurcharan. *India Unbound: The Social and Economic Revolution from Independence to the Global Information Age.* N.Y.: Anchor Books, 2002.

Desai, Neera and Thakkar, Usha. *Women in Indian Society.* New Delhi: National Book Trust, 2001.

Devasia, L. and Devasia, V.V., *The Girl Child in India.* New Delhi: Ashish Publishing House, 1991.

Diamond-Smith, Nadia, Luke, Nancy and McGarvey, Stephen. "'Too many girls, too much dowry': Son Preference and Daughter Aversion in Rural Tamil Nadu, India". *Culture, Wealth & Sexuality,* 10, No. 7 (October 2008): 697-708.

Diwan, Paras. *Family Law: Law of Marriage and Divorce in India.* New Delhi: Sterling Publishers Private Limited, 1983.

Dorow, Sarah K. *International Adoption: A Cultural Economy of Race, Gender, and Kinship.* N.Y. and London: New York University Press, 2006.

Drèze, Jean and Sen, Amartya. *An Uncertain Glory and Its Contradictions.* New Delhi: Allen Lane, 2013.

Dupony, Edmund. *Prostitution in India.* Whitefish, Montana: Kessinger Publishing, 2010.

Eldidge, Sherrie. *Twenty Things Adopted Kids Wish Their Adoptive Parents Knew.* N.Y.: Random House, 1999.

Eng, David L. *Racial Castration: Managing Masculinity in Asian America.* Durham and London: Duke University Press, 2001.

Evans, Karen. *Lost Daughters of China and the Search for a Missing Past.* N.Y.: Penguin Putnam., 2000.

Fogg-Davis, Hawley. *The Ethics of Transracial Adoption.* Ithica and London, Cornell University Press, 2002.

Fong, Mei. *One Child: The Story of China's Most Radical Experiment.* London: Clays Ltd., 2016.

Forbes, Geraldine. *Women in Modern India.* Cambridge: Cambridge University Press, 1966.

Fraschetti, Valeria. *Sari in cammino: Ecco perché l'India non è (ancora) un Paese per Donne.* Rome: Alberto Castelvecchi, 2011.

French, Patrick. *India: A Portrait.* New Delhi: Penguin Books, 2011.

Fruzzetti, Lina M. *Women, Orphans and Poverty: Social Movements and Ideologies of Work in India.* Quebec: World Heritage Press, 1998.

Fuller, Mrs. Marcus B. *The Wrongs of Indian Womanhood.* N.Y.: Revell, 1900.

Galang, M. Evelina, ed. *Screaming Monkeys: Critiques of Asian American Images.* Minneapolis, Minn.: Coffee House Press, 2001.

Gathia, J.A. *Child Prostitution in India.* New Delhi: Concept Publishing Co., 1999.

Ghurye, G.S. *Caste and Race in India.* Bombay: Popular Prakashan, 1996.

Gill, Owen and Jackson, Barbara. *Adoption & Race: Black Asian and Mixed Race Children in White Families.* N.Y.: St. Martin's Press., Inc., 1983.

Graff, E.J. "The Lie We Love", *Foreign Policy* (November/ December 2008), 59-66.

Guha, Ramachandra. *India After Gandhi: The History of the World's Largest Democracy*. London: Pan Macmillan Ltd., 2008.

Habenstein, Robert W. and Mindal, Charles H., eds. *Ethnic Families in America: Patterns and Variations*. N.Y.: Elsevier Scientific Publishing Co., 1976.

Hall, Christine. *Daughters of the Dragon: Women's Lives in Contemporary China*. London: Scarlet Press, 1997.

Harlan, Lindsay, ed. *From the Margins of Hindu Marriage: Essays on Gender, Religion and Culture*. N.Y.: Oxford University Press, 1995.

Hartmann, Betsy. *Reproductive Rights and Wrongs: The Global Politics of Population Control & Contraceptive Choice*. N.Y.: Harper & Row Publishers, 1987.

Johnson, Kay Ann. *China's Hidden Children: Abandonment, Adoption, and the Human Cost of the One-Child Policy*. Chicago: The University of Chicago Press, 2016.

———. *Wanting A Daughter, Needing A Son: Abandonment, Adoption and Orphanage Care in China*. St. Paul, Minn.: Young & Young Book Co., 2004.

———. *Women, the Family and Peasant Revolution in China*. Chicago and London: University of Chicago Press, 1983.

Hong, Maria. *Growing Up Asian American: Stories of Childhood, Adolescence and Coming of Age in America from the 1800s to the 1900s by 32 Asian American Writers*. N.Y.: Avon Books, 1993.

Human Rights Watch Children's Right Watch/Asia. *The Small Hands of Slavery*. New York, Washington, Brussels: Human Rights Watch, 1996.

India's Missing Girls. Washington D.C.: U.S. Government Printing Office, 2014.

Jha, J.K. *Status of Girl Child in India*. New Delhi: Sarup & Sons, 2002.

Kakar, Sudhir. *Indian Identity*. New Delhi: Penguin Books India Pvt. Ltd., 1996.

———. *The Indian Psyche: The Inner World Shamans, Mystics and Doctors Tales of Love, Sex and Danger.* Oxford: Oxford University Press, 1996.

———. *The Inner World: A Psychoanalytic Study of Hindu Childhood and Society.* Oxford University Press, 1983.

Kakar, Sudhir and Kakar, Katharina. *The Indians: Portrait of a People.* New Delhi: Penguin Books, 2007.

Kara, Siddharta. *Sex Trafficking: Inside the Business of Modern Slavery.* N.Y.: Columbia University Press, 2009.

Kermorgant, Catherine Rubìn. *Servants of the Goddess: The Modern Day Devadasis.* N.Y.: Vintage Books, 2014.

Kinney, Ann Behnke. *Chinese Views of Childhood.* Honolulu, Hawaii: University of Hawaii Press, 1995.

Koh, Frances M. *A China Adoption Story: Mommy, Why Do We Look Different?* Minneapolis, Minn.: East West Press, 2000.

Kusuma, A. *Status of Girl Child in India.* New Delhi: Serials Publications, 2011.

Lannoy, Richard. *The Speaking Tree: A Study of Indian Culture and Society.* New Delhi: Oxford University Press, 1974.

Lee, Robert G. *Orientals: Asian Americans in Popular Culture.* Philadelphia: Temple University Press, 1999.

Lietdke, Dr. Jane A. and Brasseur, Dr. Lee E. *New American Families: Chinese Daughters and Their Single Mothers: Adoption Stories about Hope and Love.* Bloomington, Illinois: StarNet Digital Publishing Inc., 1997.

Lifton, Betty Jean. *Lost and Found: The Adoption Experience.* Ann Arbor, Mich.: The University of Michigan Press, 2009.

———. *Twice Born: Memoirs of an Adopted Daughter.* N.Y.: St. Martin's Griffin, 1975.

Lobo, Dr. Aloma and Vasudevan, Jayapriya. *The Penguin Guide to Adoption in India.* New Delhi, Penguin Books India, 2002.

MacLeod, Jean. *At Home in this World... A China Adoption Story.* Warren, N.J.: EMK Press, 2003.

Mailer, Norman. *Cannibals and Christians.* New York: Dial Press, 1966.

Manning, Henry Edward. *Indian Child Marriages.* London: New Review, 1890.

McCormick, Patricia. *Sold.* N.Y.: Hyperion, 2006.

McKibben, Bill. *Maybe One: A Case for Smaller Families.* N.Y.: Plume, Penguin Putnam Inc., 1999.

McRoy, Ruth G. and Zurcher, Louis A. *Transracial and Inracial Adoptees: The Adolescent Years.* Springfield, Ill., 1983.

Mehadevan, K., Sumagangala, P. and Sandeep, V.M. "Gender Discrimination in China and India: Perspectives on Health, Reproduction, Survival Chances and Growth", *Gender Discrimination in Indian Society.* Edited by L. Parkian. New Delhi: Allied Publications, 2006.

Miller, Barbara D. *The Endangered Sex: Neglect of Female Children in Rural North India.* Ithica and London: Cornell University Press, 1981.

Miro, Asha. *Daughter of the Ganges: A Memoir.* N.Y.: Bantam, 2006.

Mungello, D.E. *Drowning Girls in China: Female Infanticide since 1650.* Plymouth, U.K.: Rowman and Littlefield Publishers, Inc., 2008.

Nagaseshamma, S. *Street Children of India: A Socio-Legal Study.* New Delhi: Anmol Publications Pvt. Ltd., 2010.

Nagi, B. *Child Marriage in India. A Study of its Differential Patterns in Rajasthan.* Udaipur: Mittal Publications, 1993.

Natayam, Balmurli and Greenough, Paul, eds. *Against Stigma: Studies in Caste, Race, and Justice since Durban.* New Delhi: Orient Blackswan, 2009.

Patton, Sandra. *Birthmarks: Transracial Adoption in Contemporary America.* N.Y. and London: New York University Press, 2000.

Palumbo-Lin, David. *Asian/American: Historical Crossings of a Racial Frontier.* Stanford, Calif.: Stanford University Press, 1999.

Penzer, N.M. *Poison Damsels and Other Essays in Folklore and Anthropology.* London: Chas J. Sawyer, 1952.

Rauhala, Ann, ed. *The Lucky Ones: Our Stories of Adopting Children from China.* Toronto, Ontario: New Press, 2008.

Rojewski, Jay W. and Rojewski, Jacy L. *Intercountry Adoption from China: Examining Cultural Heritage and Other Postadoption Issues.* Westport, Conn. and London: Bergin & Garvey, 2001.

Reddy, Narayan. *Marriages in India.* Gurgaon: The Academic Press, 1978.

Ross, A.D. *The Hindu Family in Its Urban Setting.* Toronto: University of Toronto Press, 1961.

Rothman, Barbara Katz. *Weaving a Family: Untangling Race and Adoption.* Boston, Mass.: Beacon Press Books, 1992.

Rush, Sharon E. *Loving Across the Color Line: A White Adoptive Mother Learns about Race.* N.Y.: Rowman Littlefield Publishers, Inc., 2000.

Sagade, Jaya. *Child Marriage in India: Socio-Legal and Human Rights Dimensions.* New Delhi: Oxford University Press, 2005.

Sahni, Rohini, ed. *Prostitution and Beyond: An Analysis of Sex Workers in India.* New Delhi: Sage Publications, 2008.

Schaefer, Carol. *The Other Mother: A Woman's Love for the Child She Gave Up for Adoption.* N.Y.: Soho Press, Inc., 1991.

Sen, Anima and Seth, Salma. "Gender identity of the girl child in South Asia". *Canadian Human Studies,* 15, No. 2/3 (Spring/Summer 1955), 58-63.

Sherwani, Azim. *The Girl Child in Crisis.* New Delhi: Indian Social Institute, 1998.

Simon, Rita J. and Altstein, Howard. *Adoption Across Borders: Serving the Children in Transracial and Intercountry Adoptions.* N.Y. and Lanham, Md.: Rowman & Littlefield Publishers, Inc., 2000.

Sinha, S.N. *History of Marriage and Prostitution in India.* New Delhi: Khama Publishers, 1992.

Smolin, David. "The Two Faces of Intercountry Adoption: The Significance on the Indian Adoption Scandals". *Seton Hall Review* 35, No. 2 (2005), 403-93.

Srinivas, M.N. *Caste in Modern India And Other Essays.* London: Asia Publishing House, 1962.

———. *Marriage and Family in Mysore.* Bombay: New Book Co., 1942.

Srinivasan, Sharada and Bedi, Arjun S. "Ensuring Daughter Survival in Tamil Nadu, India." *Oxford Development Studies* 39, No. 3 (September, 2011), 253-83.

Sumner, Molly M. "The unknown genocide: How one country's culture is destroying the girl child". *International Journal of Nursing Practice* 15 (2009), 65-68.

Takaki, Ronald. *Strangers from a Different Shore: A History of Asian Americans.* N.Y.: Penguin Books USA Inc., 1989.

Tan, Pamela. *The Chinese Factor: An Australian Chinese Woman's Life in China from 1950 to 1979.* Kenthurst, Australia: Rosenberg, 2008.

———. *Women in Society: China.* N.Y., London, Sydney: Marshall Cavendish, 1993.

Tessler, Richard, Gamachee, Gail and Liu, Liming. *West Meets East: Americans Adopt Chinese Children.* Westport, Conn. and London, 1999.

Tripathy, S.N. and Pradhan, S.P. *Girl Child in India.* New Delhi: Discovery Publishing House, 2003.

Trenka, Jane Jeong, Oparah, Julia Chinyere and Shin, Sun Yung. *Outsiders Within: Writing on Transracial Adoption.* Cambridge, Mass.: South End Press, 2006.

Varma, Pavan K. *Becoming Indian: The Unfinished Revolution of Culture and Identity*. New Delhi: Penguin Books India Pvt. Ltd., 2010.

———. *Being Indian: The Truth about Why the Twenty-First Century will be India's*. New York: Viking, 2004.

———. *Chanakya's New Manifesto to Resolve the Crisis Within India*. New Delhi: Aleph Book Company, 2013.

Verrier, Nancy Newton. *The Primal Wound: Understanding the Adopted Child*. Baltimore, Md: Gateway Press, Inc., 2015.

Wolf, Arthur P. and Huang, Chieh-shan. *Marriage and Adoption in China, 1845-1945*. Stanford, Calif.: Stanford University Press, 1980.

Wolf, Margery. *Revolution Postponed: Women in Contemporary China*. Stanford, Calif.: Stanford University Press, 1985.

Wolff, Jana. *Secret Thoughts of an Adoptive Mother*. Honolulu, Hawaii: Vista Communications, 1999.

Xinran. *The Good Women of China: Hidden Voices*. London: Vintage, 2001.

NEWSPAPERS AND MAGAZINES

"A case for lifting burdens of India's poor", *International Herald Tribune*, September 7-8, 2013, 22.

"Children who Sell Themselves", *International Herald Tribune*, September 7, 2011, 8.

"First set of parents post government's foster care norms can't name kids", *The Indian Express*, July 2, 2017, http://indianexpress.com/article/india/first-set-of-parents-post-governments-foster-care-norms-cant-name-kids-4731651/

"India becoming hub for child prostitution", *The Times of India*, January 30, 2010, https://timesofindia.indiatimes.com/india/India-becoming-hub-for-child-prostitution/articleshow/5514551.cms

"United in grief, farmers lament loss of children 'stolen' by officials", *South China Morning Post*, March 21, 2006, http://www.scmp.com/article/541264/united-grief-farmers-lament-loss-children-stolen-officials

"Village moral codes follow Indian women studying in cities." *International Herald Tribune*, October 21, 2013, 1-7.

"Where are the baby girls?" *International Herald Tribune*, September, 3, 2010, 6.

Ali, Sayed Intishab. "Now, Tracking Device to curb foeticide", *The Times of India*, May 15, 2012, 1.

Aravamudan, Gita, "Child trafficking, 'manufactured orphans': The dark underbelly of inter-country adoption in India", *Firstpost*, September 3, 2017, https://www.firstpost.com/india/child-trafficking-manufactured-orphans-the-dark-underbelly-of-inter-country-adoption-in-india-4000837.html

Barnagarwala, Tabassum, Before the Baby Goes Home", *The Indian Express*, September 13, 2016, http://indianexpress.com/article/lifestyle/life-style/foster-care-in-india-model-guidelines-by-ministry-of-women-and-child-development-adoption-3024715/

Bathial, Vimal, "'Save girl child' monogram to dot all letters in Jaisalmer". *The Times of India*, Jaipur, May 15, 2012, 3.

Bedi, Arjun S. and Srinivasan, Sharada, "Girl Child protection Scheme in Tamil Nadu: An Appraisal", *Economical & Political Weekly*, Vol. 44, Issue No. 48, November 28, 2009, http://www.epw.in/journal/2009/48/commentary/girl-child-protection-scheme-tamil-nadu-appraisal.html

Beech, Hannah, "China's Baby Traffickers", *Time*, January 8, 2001, http://www.time.com/time/asia/magazine/2001/0108/babies.smuggle.html

———, "Court Convicts 52 of Baby-Trafficking in China", *The New York Times*, July 7, 2004, http://www.nytimes.com/2004/07/24/world/court-convicts-52-of-baby-trafficking-in-china.html

Bhavika, Jain, "Dads of newborn girls to get free shave here", *The Times of India*, New Delhi, January 16, 2017, 15.

Ford, Rebecca, "Child Victims Make Up 40 Percent of India's Prostitutes", *The Hollywood Reporter*, December 2015, 64-66, https://ramonabraganza.com/wp-content/uploads/2015/11/THR_WIE_Braganza.pdf

Gettleman, Jeffrey and Kumar, Hari, "India Shields Child Brides From Sex", *The New York Times*, October 11, 2017, https://www.nytimes.com/2017/10/11/world/asia/india-child-marriage-rape.html

Kannampilly, Ammu, "'Culture of abuse' at India's children's care homes", *The National*, July 15, 2012, https://www.thenational.ae/world/asia/culture-of-abuse-at-india-s-children-s-care-homes-1.457713

LaFraniere, Sharon, "Chinese Officials Seized and Sold Babies, Parents Say", *The New York Times*, August 4, 2011, https://www.nytimes.com/2011/08/05/world/asia/05kidnapping.html

Mohanty, Ranjani I., "Trash Bin Babies: India's female Infanticide Crisis", *The Atlantic*, May 25, 2012, https://www.theatlantic.com/international/archive/2012/05/trash-bin-babies-indias-female-infanticide-crisis/257672/

Rahman, Shaikh Azizur, "Indian children stolen for adoption", *The National*, June 29, 2010, https://www.thenational.ae/world/asia/indian-children-stolen-for-adoption-1.539489

———, "Tragic plight of India's young temple girls", *The National*, March 19, 2010, https://www.thenational.ae/world/asia/tragic-plight-of-india-s-young-temple-girls-1.599285

Townsend, Mark, "The scandal of the missing children abducted from India's railway stations", *The Guardian*, July 30, 2017, https://www.theguardian.com/global-development/2017/jul/30/global-development-india-child-trafficking

WEBSITES

"India abortion: Police find 19 female fetuses", *BBC News*, March 6, 2017, http://www.bbc.com/news/world-asia-india-39176668

"Investigation of Delhi orphanage reveals tale of sexual abuse and violence", *NDTV*, February 11, 2012, https://www.ndtv.com/delhi-news/investigation-of-delhi-orphanage-reveals-tale-of-sexual-abuse-and-violence-572729

Agrawal, Shaifali, "Cradles in Rajasthan for India's unwanted babies", *Al Jazeera*, December 26, 2016, https://www.aljazeera.com/indepth/features/2016/12/cradles-rajasthan-india-unwanted-babies-161205080218497.html

Anteleva, Natalia, "The girls stolen from the streets of India", *BBC World Service, Delhi*, January 9, 2013, http://www.bbc.com/news/magazine-20938125

Banerjee, Chandana, "Prakash Kaur Bibi: Rescuing India's abandoned girls", *Al Jazeera*, July 17, 2016, https://www.aljazeera.com/indepth/features/2016/06/prakash-kaur-bibi-rescuing-india-abandoned-girls-160606093358320.html

Bhalla, Nita, "India's cradle baby scheme hopes to end female infanticide", *Reuters*, December 3, 2013, https://www.reuters.com/article/us-india-cradlebabies/indias-cradle-baby-scheme-hopes-to-end-female-infanticide-idUSBRE9B206P20131203

Colundalur, Nash, "Devadasis are a cursed community", *The Guardian*, January 21, 2011, https://www.theguardian.com/lifeandstyle/2011/jan/21/devadasi-india-sex-work-religion

Deshpande, Haima, "Using minors in prostitution is a billion dollar industry in the city", *DNA India*, March 9, 2007, http://www.dnaindia.com/mumbai/report-using-minors-in-prostitution-is-a-billion-dollar-industry-in-the-city-1083952

Dhody, Tarini, "Abandoned and Unwanted: Child Adoption Rates Fall By 50% In India", *ScoopWhoop*, April 22, 2015, https://www.scoopwhoop.com/news/adopt-a-child/#.ss1rgcz3p

Goldman, Russell, "An Adoption Nightmare", *abcNEWS*, May 14, 2000, http://abcnews.go.com/International/story?id=4823713&page=1

Gottlieb, Benjamin and Frost, Emily, "In India, non-Hindu parents face adoption prejudice", *Dawn*, July 30, 2012, https://www.dawn.com/news/738379

Johari, Aarefa, "As Modi launches another girl child scheme, here's why previous initiatives in the area failed", *Scroll.in*, January 23, 2015, https://scroll.in/article/701730/as-modi-launches-another-girl-child-scheme-heres-why-previous-initiatives-in-the-area-failed

Kalra, Aparna, "Why Only 3.2% Of India's 50,000 Orphans Will Find Parents", *IndiaSpend*, March 5, 2016, http://www.indiaspend.com/cover-story/why-only-3-2-of-indias-50000-orphans-will-find-parents-34599

Kannan, Shilpa, "Child labour: India's hidden shame", *BBC News, Delhi*, February 5, 2014, http://www.bbc.com/news/business-25947984

Nagaraj, Anuradha, "Cradle baby scheme across India: Legitimising traditional discrimination against girl child?", *The News Minute*, July 19, 2014, https://www.thenewsminute.com/lives/92

"Orphanage shut down for selling babies in eastern India", *Thomson Reuters Foundation News*, February 21, 2017, https://news.trust.org/item/20170221145057-1bwob/

Salian, Priti, "India's 'dark holes' where millions of girls disappear", *Al Jazeera*, December 17, 2015, https://www.aljazeera.com/indepth/features/2015/12/india-dark-holes-millions-girls-disappear-151203073343634.html

Vishakh, Unnikrishnan, "Delhi UC slams Central Adoption Agency, blames it for low adoption rates", 20 July, 2016, CatchNews, www.catchnews.com/india-news/

PERSONAL INTERVIEWS

Shashimoni. Personal Interview, October 23, 2011.

UNIVERSITY STUDIES

Kapoor, R. "A Sociological Study of Adoption with Special Reference to India" M.A. Thesis. University of Delhi, 1996.